"DON'T HIT MY MAMA!"

OVERCOMING THE EFFECTS OF CHILDHOOD DOMESTIC VIOLENCE

"DON'T HIT MY MAMA!"

OVERCOMING THE EFFECTS OF CHILDHOOD DOMESTIC VIOLENCE

RENESIA MARTIN

CHILDHOOD DOMESTIC VIOLENCE WITNESS AND SURVIVOR

RECOVERY &
WHOLENESS BOOKS

OMAHA, NEBRASKA

Disclaimer: The intent of the author is to offer information to help you in your journey for mental, emotional and spiritual well-being. In the event you use any of the information in this book or website for yourself, neither the author nor publisher assumes any responsibility for your actions.

Paperback ISBN: 978-0-9882048-2-9
Kindle ISBN: 978-0-9882048-3-6
ePub ISBN: 978-0-9882048-4-3

LCCN: 2012915120

"Characteristics of a Batterer" on page 205 has been used with permission from the South Carolina Coalition Against Domestic Violence and Sexual Assault

Don't Hit My Mama!
Published by:
Recovery & Wholeness Books LLC

www.RenesiaMartin.com

Book cover design by Floyd Orfield
Author's photograph taken by Christi Brew at Lifehouse Photography
10   9   8   7   6   5   4   3

DEDICATION

Foremost, I dedicate this book to my heavenly Father, my Lord and Savior Jesus Christ, and the Holy Spirit, who never gave up on me.

To my beloved brother Lorenzo and parents, Hillie Martin and Lillian Rush: Thank you for being there to support and encourage me through the process of healing and wholeness.

Finally, I dedicate this book to each and every child, woman, or man who has witnessed or experienced family violence. I love you and pray if you have not found wholeness and healing, that today you will begin your journey.

ACKNOWLEDGMENTS

This is one of the most difficult pages to write because I have had so many people who have been instrumental in helping me throughout my life, and I do not think this form of acknowledgment does them justice. Therefore, I consider this just the beginning and not a once and done thing.

First of all, I want to thank the God of the Universe and the Holy Spirit who prompted me to write about this important subject. Second, I want to thank my brother Lorenzo for standing by me when we were growing up and while I wrote this book. I am also very grateful for both my mother and father who throughout the process of my writing this book, never once discouraged me to stop. In fact, they both provided me with on-going support to continue forward. Without their support I would not have had the courage to disclose some of our family secrets. Third, I honor and adore my pastors, Drs. Martin and Lynnell Williams, for their dedication, commitment and loyalty to the Kingdom of God. As role models, they have provided me with the encouragement and support to push forward toward my destiny, calling and purpose in life.

Fourth, a very special thank you goes to Dr. Jimmie Reed for her coaching, encouragement, fortitude, leadership, guidance and advice over the past ten years of my life. You have been there when I could not get my wagon in gear or my head on straight, saying, "Come on; you can make it. You are coming out of this mess!" You never let me go or gave up on me, and for this I am eternally grateful.

All along life's journey I have been fortunate and blessed to have wise, skilled and gifted ministers, pastors, teachers, coaches, psychotherapists, psychologists and friends who were central to my process of finding healing and wholeness. The following people have played significant key roles in my healing and restoration: Dr. Judy and Joe Fornara, Dr. Dorothy Blaylark-Hill, Earl and Sara Watson, Dr. Patricia Fancher, Dr. Douglas Weiss, Cheryl Field and Peter Brewer, friend and Coach Tanya Warren, Coach Connie Yori, Coach Bruce Rasmussen and my dear friend of twenty years, Crystal McDaniel.

Lastly, but certainly not least, I can never adequately thank my formal and informal editors, Dr. Bruce Cook, Erin Zimmer, Peggy Spiller, and the Bryant Family (Paul, Robin, Brazier, Paul Jr., and Madison.)

AUTHOR'S NOTES

In this memoir, I have recounted events and conversations to the very best of my memory. Where my recollections are less complete, I have tried to present events and conversations as best as possible how I recalled them. Some details are not complete, only because they are snippets or impressions in my mind and memory.

I have changed some names, locations and identifying details of individuals to protect their privacy; however, the vast majority of names, locations and details of events that occurred are actually factual.

DEFINITIONS

WITNESS[1]

1: attestation of a fact or event: testimony

2: one that gives evidence; specifically: one who testifies in a cause or before a judicial tribunal

3: one who has personal knowledge of something

SURVIVOR[2]

1: to remain alive or in existence : live on

2: to continue to function or prosper

transitive verb

3: to continue to function or prosper despite : withstand <they survived many hardships>

---

1   www.merriam-webster.com/dictionary/witness, 11/28/08
2   www.merriam-webster.com/dictionary/survivor, 11/28/08

CONTENTS

ENDORSEMENTS

Don't Hit My Mama!

There are many who have lived in and witnessed abusive relationships and feel no one else understands their pain or perspective. *"How could anyone believe me and understand why I see life as I do?"* Many do not even realize what life has been stolen from them, or what healthy families and relationships look like.

In this book that depicts riveting and at times dramatic experiences, Renesia Martin has captured the essence of what it is to have witnessed a lifestyle of family abuse and not only to have survived, but been able to come into *real freedom from the resulting bondage and dysfunction that ensues from such abuse.*

If you have lived a lifestyle of abuse and desire to face what it takes to become free and whole, this is a must read. Renesia captures the very heart of what people need in order to become emotionally and spiritually healed and to find God's plan and purpose for their future.

Dr. Jimmie Reed, Senior Leader
Revelation International/Revolution Global Center

This is a riveting perspective of a life shaped and molded by circumstances but also a life that found its way back to destiny! This book has taken me on a journey and has brought me, and should bring every reader, back to the reality that experiences like this are the real testimonies of so many others. We cannot afford to ignore any of them. But I see great healing in the "wings" (pages) of this book and this great author will undoubtedly save and heal many lives through her writing. Great work!

Dr. Gordon E. Bradshaw, Author, Trainer, Network President,
Apostolic Leader, Global Effect Movers & Shakers Network

FOREWORD

I recommend this book to victims, counselors, pastors, and lay leaders who want to help families heal from their cycles of abuse. I have counseled hundreds of people through the years, and I am keenly aware of the devasting consequences of abuse to the human heart. The disharmony of the soul is expressed in plaguing doubts, painful memories, physical injuries, family stress, unforgiveness toward others, and unforgivable sins. Literally millions of people in our world today have suffered from domestic violence and physical, emotional and/or sexual abuse. When the mind, heart, and spirit aren't whole, we become hurting people who hurt people. Therefore, generational patterns of abuse continue until the brave victims and witnesses choose to speak up, work through their painful memories and receive healing.

This is a remarkable book about domestic violence as told in this eyewitness account by the daughter, now an adult woman. The journey is told from the perspective of a frightened child who was the victim of abuse and witnessed the abuse of her mother. She tells how that abuse traumatized her childhood and how she stopped feeling. She stuffed those painful thoughts and feelings into an internal black box to survive and dealt with life by taking charge, working hard and trying to please others.

Throughout this book you will see how God has kept and protected Lillian, the children, and even Hillie. None of the counseling sessions would have been successful without the power of the Holy Spirit working in and through all those present. Faith and obedience to God changed the abuser, making the intense family counseling sessions productive and healing for those he had abused. Faith enabled Lillian to leave, protecting both herself and her children. Faith in Jesus Christ helped Lorenzo and Renesia to overcome their childhood trauma, do the right things, make better choices than their parents, and become the adults who God wanted them to become. The generational cycles of abuse have been broken as has drug abuse, adultery, domestic violence and poverty by their courage to change.

Their journey will inspire others to seek the help of a skilled therapist, break the silence and reveal inner secrets that are locked deep within wounded hearts. A lifetime of freedom and healing are worth the brief pain. Breaking the cycle of abuse will free you as well as your children and grandchildren. I feel privileged to have worked with Renesia and her family in their journey to heal from the abuse. I am so proud of Lillian, Hillie, Lorenzo and Renesia for taking time out of their busy lives to work through the painful memories and open up old wounds, cleaning them out rather than covering them up.

Martin Luther King Jr. once said: "Take the first step in Faith. You don't have to see the whole staircase; just take the first step." That is what happens all along this family's journey. Each person individually stepped out in faith one step at a time until all could receive the healing God had for them. If they had looked only at their circumstances, they would have felt defeated and hopeless, but they looked at the Creator of the Universe, God Almighty, who can do far greater things then we can ever imagine or hope. Perhaps buying and reading this book is your first step in Faith.

May God help you work through your own journey to healing. Perhaps you know a victim who needs to read this book. Buy it, read it yourself, and then encourage that person to begin their faith walk to heal.

Patricia Fancher, LMFT, Ph.D

INTRODUCTION

Do you know someone who has witnessed domestic violence? Are you a survivor of domestic violence? Personally, I want you to know you are not alone. I spent the first thirty-three years of my life trying to run and hide from past pain and struggles, consciously unaware there were traumatic events which I had placed in a black box inside the attic of my mind. The box was locked and no one was given access. On the outside of the box were warning labels -- familiar warnings like Danger Ahead, No Access, Dead End, and Explosive Materials Inside.

On another front, I had a secondary battle going on. Sometimes I was consciously or unconsciously bombarded with negative thoughts such as: "You are worthless and unloveable; you must prove you are loveable; you must prove you have worth and value; you don't fit in; blend into the woodwork; just don't think or talk about what happened; pretend like it never happened; no one else has to know; this is family; and don't give away the family secrets." Another stream of my thought patterns flowed like this: "If people really knew what had happened, they would reject you and think you are crazy. People will come to the conclusion you deserve it because you really are WORTH-LESS."

All the while the black box was in command and controlling me more than I ever thought. Shortly after my 33rd birthday, I hit a brick wall. I was at the height of my corporate career. At this juncture in my career I was experiencing more success than I could have imagined and placed in a position of influence. I had access to high levels of leaders within the organization I worked for. Yet, I was discontent. There was an emptiness and void on the inside nothing or no one could fill. I was no longer comfortable in my current mental state of being.

Finally, I had to run to the black box inside my mind and begin to pull out the trauma I had hidden so deep inside. For those who dare to come, join me on my journey as we explore in greater detail those trauma triggers which held me captive for so long. This is a call out to the silent victims. We must break the silence. It is an open invitation for those of us who are willing to face our deepest fears, and to begin our own journey to wholeness.

On our journey, we move from a place of being victims to a place of being a witness. It is our time to expose the truth and share our story. I am a witness! You may be a witness or know of a witness to domestic violence. Be daring enough to share your painful experiences so you can heal from the shame and deep sense of loneliness which have bound so many of us. Our trauma triggers may be different. No matter what, I encourage you to face and embrace the past so you do not have to repeat the cycle of abuse, or carry shackles and chains into your future.

In this book, I will uncover and expose a number of the items which were hidden in my internal black box. Also, I will share the methods I used to face my own demons. I am convinced that if we do not face our demons they will continually haunt us. In some form or fashion they will appear as tormentors. There is no escaping our tormentors. Believe me, I tried to escape. The harder I tried to escape, the more it seems I ran to that which I was trying to escape from.

As children, our ways of coping may have provided some comfort for us, but as adults they keep us caught in dysfunctional relationships, wrong belief systems, and destructive thought patterns. Occasionally, these ways of coping are camouflaged as cycles of abuse or addictive behaviors. Sometimes we may even sabotage our own success and develop habits of self-mutilation in an attempt to escape pain.

I must warn you. Before you commit to reading what's on the inside of this book, prepare yourself mentally, spiritually and emotionally. If you were a witness to domestic violence or have experienced domestic violence, then reading this book could potentially ignite or trigger unhealed hurts and pain. If you get to a place or point where you want to cry, take the time to cry. Stop reading and allow your tears to flow and bring healing in your life. You may need to call a close friend and share what you are feeling. It is possible you may need to seek out a licensed therapist, psychologist, psychotherapist, Christian counselor, self-help material, support group and/or a minister who is gifted and/or trained in the area of inner healing and deliverance. I encourage you to do whatever it takes to deal with the demons which have plagued so many of our lives.

I want you to know that the God of the Universe has heard our cries as children witnessing domestic violence. Additionally, the cries of victims and perpetrators have been heard as well. The cries were so loud that I heard them and it was impressed upon my heart to write this book.

The message I bring to those who have been in or witnessed domestic violence is that we are loved and not alone. Secondly, this book has been written so that others will have an increased understanding and awareness of the impact that witnessing domestic violence has on children. "Watching parents hit each other has the same psychological effect on children as if they were beaten themselves," said Joy O'Banion, director of the Family Support and Treatment Center in Orem, UT.[3] Thirdly, the God of the Universe and I want you to know whatever trauma you experienced in the past does not have to continue to hinder your future. If you are in a situation where you are currently experiencing domestic violence, know most importantly, you CAN COME OUT! You can be a catalyst to break the cycle of abuse and dysfunction, and to be a witness.

> *I am convinced; if we do not face our demons they will continually haunt us as victims. In some form or fashion they will appear, disappear and reappear as tormentors.*

---

3   Dennis Romboy and Lucinda Dillon Kinkead, *Silent victims: Kids who witness abuse face psychological woes.*

Lorenzo (age 7) and Renesia Martin (age 5)

PART ONE

HIDDEN INSIDE THE "BLACK BOX"

WHAT HAPPENED?

CHAPTER ONE
FAMILY SECRETS BROUGHT TO LIGHT

What happens at home stays at home. This is family.

Typically, when we meet new people, we start by listing our accomplishments. We say where we went to college, what we do for work, where we live, or maybe even the size of our home. This is a different kind of conversation – a conversation about what is hidden away—the family secrets that destroy us as individuals, as families, and as a society.

While growing up, I was a witness to domestic violence. This was one of my family's darkest secrets. Not my teachers, not even my dearest friends, knew what was going on behind closed doors in our home. There was an unwritten code of silence—a code which I never broke. Only our closest family members knew, and even with them, I never told them what happened. I never said what I saw with my eyes, what I heard with my ears, what I thought with my mind, or what I felt with my emotions. I did not disclose my inner world to anyone. I kept those secrets hidden deep inside of me. Some of those memories and feelings were hidden so deep that not even I could access them. They had all gone into my little black box, a place unconsciously created in my mind to protect me from all the terror I experienced by hiding the truth from myself. Memories and experiences went in and did not come back out.

Until now….

It was 1973 – the year abortions became a constitutional right in the United States (Roe v. Wade). The year Watergate hearings began. I was five. My brother Lorenzo was seven. On the surface we appeared like a normal family on a hot summer night. While our Mom finished cleaning the kitchen, we sat playing on the bedroom floor of our apartment on the south side of Chicago. Lorenzo played with his match box metal cars, rolling them back and forth while I rocked my favorite doll, Tamu. I loved my Tamu doll because she could talk. I pulled her short string at the middle of her back. She responded with a sweet, "Tell me a story." I smiled and hugged her tightly.

Mom came into the room and told us it was time for bed. My brother put on his royal blue Spiderman pajamas and I put on my pink princess gown, and the three of us got on our knees to say our nightly prayers.

> *Now I lay me down to sleep, I pray the Lord my soul to keep; if I should die before I wake, I pray the Lord my soul to take. God, please bless Mama, Daddy, Grandma Maeomia, Grandpa Clarence...*

After praying, we climbed into our beds. My Mom tucked us in, kissed our foreheads, and turned off the overhead light. A night light kept the room slightly illuminated. Another night light in the hallway was already turned on, making our pathway to the bathroom well lit. My Mom started to close the door but I asked, "Mom, please leave the door open." She smiled gently and left the door cracked.

I settled into bed and thought about the day. We had had a good day. There was a quietness and peacefulness in the atmosphere. Dad was not home. We had not seen or heard from him for several days. The last time I had talked to him and asked him where he was, he had said he was at work. In my mind, I thought Dad lived at work because he was there more than he was at home. Our apartment was quiet except for the familiar creaking of floors in the hallway and low sound of cars passing by our apartment on the street outside. I drifted off to sleep.

Abruptly I was awakened by the loud sounds of yelling, screaming, wrestling, and tumbling. The roomed seemed more darkened and I could feel terror in the atmosphere. I thought to myself, Oh, no! Dad is home. I felt afraid. I called for my brother. He was still fast asleep. "Get up, get up!" I yelled, "Dad's here!"

My parents married young. Mom was eighteen years old and fresh out of high school. The oldest of nine children (five girls and four boys), Mom was ready to get out of the house upon graduation. She had hopes of going to college, getting married, and having a large family. Mom excelled in school and graduated near the top of her class. She had received applications from her guidance counselor for colleges in the area. Excited, she took the applications home to her parents. She introduced the idea to them about furthering her education. They explained they just could not afford it. They were very proud to have their first high school graduate.

Mom was ten years old when the family moved north from Little Rock, Arkansas to Chicago, Illinois. Chicago was considered to be the land of opportunity. Mom was always beautiful. She had a dark brown completion, pleasant smile, and a shapely figure. She was mild mannered, kind, and merciful to everyone she met.

Originally from Arkansas, Mom's parents, Clarence and Maeomia, had been share- croppers. They had picked cotton and worked farmland their whole lives. While they lived in the south there was still a large degree of discrimination and segregation. Many African Americans sought a better life by moving to Northern states between 1910 and 1970. This was considered The Great Migration. It was an exciting time to leave the South.

Mom's father, Clarence, moved to Chicago first. He had found gainful employment working in a factory. After working for a number of months, he saved enough money to move the family. He was tired of the hard labor of the South. They received minimal pay for sharecropping. He had experienced many injustices in the South. He vowed his children would not experience the same.

As a child, Grandpa Clarence appeared to be larger than life. He was handsome with chocolate brown skin. He stood six feet, four inches tall and wore a size fifteen shoe. In the South, landowners would have described him as a "big black buck" because of his size, strength, and skin completion. When he left the South, the landowners were not happy about his departure and attempted to persuade him into staying.

As grandkids we were always fearful of Grandpa. His voice was thunderous. His hands were so big they could cover your whole face and head. He could slap both of your legs at the same time in one swoop, front and back. We stayed quiet when he was around.

Maeomia was beautiful with light golden-brown skin. She stood five feet, eight inches in height. She seemed like a tower in comparison to other women. She was a no nonsense lady who would not take anything from anyone, except Grandpa. There was something about Maeomia's presence that commanded respect and authority. Even though she lived in a rough neighborhood, she never once had a problem with anyone attempting to bother her. She was a hard-working lady who possessed much wisdom and strength. Her love was tender and genuine. With her voice and smile she could touch your heart. There was always a safe place to run and hide behind her dress.

Mom's closest friends were a small group of girls from her neighborhood. She spent most of her time with her girlfriends. They would get together to go to dances, movies, or just to hang out. Sometimes they would meet up with a group of guys and attend events. That's how Mom and Dad met. Mom's group of friends met up with a group of guys and started hanging out together. They would meet at different apartments in the low income Robert Taylor housing project where they all lived. As a large group they spent time listening to music, laughing, and playing card games and having fun.

Dad was the life of the party. He always had the latest music and knew the words to every love song. His singing voice was beautiful. He was two years older than Mom. When they met he already had his own apartment. He worked for a local grocery store and even had his own car. He was very handsome, fun, charismatic, meticulous, and well-groomed. Supposedly he had graduated from high school. But he never really did. Dad could barely read or write. He never made it past the seventh grade.

Both of my Dad's parents were from the South as well. His mother, Kathleen was from Tennessee and Hewitt, his father was from Louisiana. Kathleen was a single parent most of her life. She was a beautiful lady inside and out. She had golden-brown skin and eyes that danced. Her inner beauty was more visible than her outer beauty. She was kind, gentle, and merciful. Kathleen would hardly speak above a whisper. She was seventeen years old when she married Hewitt who was forty-four years old. I am told that Hewitt was a very mean man.

Dad never had the opportunity to meet or even see a picture of his father. Hewitt was so abusive that Kathleen had no contact with him. Her family had forbidden Hewitt from seeing her. They moved her into their home and did everything they could to protect her.

Unfortunately, Hewitt died mysteriously when Dad was two or three years old. His body was found decapitated on the railroad tracks. It was not clear whether his body was placed on the railroad tracks after being murdered, or if he committed suicide.

Growing up, Dad would often ask his mother for a description of his father. Grandma Kathleen would respond, "If you want to see him, look in the mirror."

Dad was born in Chicago. He grew up in a family of five children. He was the middle child. He had two older brothers and two younger sisters. Oddly enough, each of the five children had a different father. Dad's family was very poor. He started work by selling clothes hangers, shining shoes, or doing odd jobs when he was around ten years old. They hardly had enough food to eat, so Dad thought working was more important than education.

Dad witnessed some domestic violence in his home but it was less severe and frequent than the violence my mother witnessed in her home. On the other hand, my father experienced abuse and violence as a victim at a much more extreme level than my mother. Dad's side of the family was less functional than Mom's family. He experienced neglect at a heightened level. His most basic needs of safety, security, food, clothing, and shelter were not consistently met.

In both households, customary rules of the South were used to rear the children, meaning, children were to be seldom seen and never heard. It also meant disciplinary action and punishment which would be considered child abuse today. Both of my parents have spoken and given accounts of being spanked or beaten with extension cords, broom handles, and whatever else could be found nearby to inflict pain. If children were out of reach, there was always the option of throwing boomerang shoes or other objects at them.

There was so much abuse that took place at home that Mom grew up thinking abuse was normal. In addition to the children being physically abused occasionally, Grandma Maeomia was physically abused by Grandpa Clarence.

In hindsight, there were traces of violence back to my great grandparents on my mother's side of the family. Prior to Grandma Maeomia passing away, she told me her father was a very abusive man. She went on to say that her mother died mysteriously. She believed her father had possibly poisoned her mother. She was not willing to take this secret to the grave with her. This was a family secret I kept for her.

Grandpa Clarence said his dad was meek and humble and was not a violent man. In contrast, his mother was just the opposite. She was actually the abusive and violent one. She was close to six feet tall and very intimidating. She ruled the house and everyone in it. He said, "She was the meanest lady you would ever want to meet." His parents grew up being overseers of some of the sharecroppers. His mom was good at keeping everyone on task and in line. Grandpa Clarence said he was even afraid of her.

Grandma Kathleen passed away when I was twelve years old. Sorry to say, I was not able to get as much history regarding my great grandparents on her side of the family. Since we never met Hewitt or any of his family members, I was not able to get his family history of violence either.

Chapter Two
Hung From The
Balcony

Until I was thirty-three, I was in agreement with my subconscious mind and the little black box. I wanted and tried as hard as I could to keep the memories of what had happened in my childhood out of my mind. I did not want to talk or think about what had transpired. I did not want to feel the feelings, or own the emotions, associated with much of my childhood and adolescence. I erected walls to hide and protect them. I wanted all of those traumatic incidents and memories to remain hidden and undiscoverable. I pretended like they had never happened and reasoned that if I did not think about them or let them play out in my mind, then maybe they really did not occur. I fooled everyone but myself.

On this night there was a new shifting that took place in my mind. I was no longer limited by the boundaries of my conscious mind. I was no longer limited by reality but found a place of safety in another realm, the realm of my imagination. I closed my eyes to the light of the world outside of myself -- reality with all its limits and boundaries. My mind opened to the darkness on the inside of me. In the darkness of my imagination there were no more boundaries. I was no longer limited by reality. Imagination, disassociation, denial, and a sense of powerfulness were discovered. These were my escape routes and captors where I learned to hide deep inside of me. Stepping out of reality and entering into an inner world of darkness gave me the ability to survive trauma.

When I attempt to recall that night in its entirety, scenes appear, disappear, transition in and out like a surreal movie in my mind. At times, the movie screen goes black. I can remember some scenes in my heart but not picture them clearly in my mind; instead, they are just snippets, impressions of moments. In my heart, I know exactly what happened, but my little black box has removed parts of the night from my conscious mind forever. However, I can recall in detail the emotions and feelings from this event. Looking back, I remember the terror and hysteria I felt. I can hear sounds—yelling, screaming, sirens blaring, and an ambulance door slamming shut. I hear Mom's cry for help. I hear my cry for help. It was a painful night. My mind wants me to forget it, but my memories and feelings will not allow it.

"My dad is beating up my mom; please come and help us." We had made this call many times before. Whenever something was going awry, we called family members for help. They were our first line of defense. No one taught us to do this. We just knew we needed help. We knew we had family members who supported and loved us, and had come to our rescue many times before. Grandma Maeomia's house was less than a mile away. We lived on 68th and Halsted and my "granny" lived on 56th and Carpenter. I do not remember that fateful night if I dialed the number or if my brother dialed. Like a part of my own being, I remember us saying our routine, "My Dad is beating up my Mom; please come and help us." But this night would be different than other nights. Even though they would come to help, it would be too late for the worst of the tragedy.

One day as I was sifting through these memories, it hit me like a ton of bricks: "Where was my older brother when things were out of control?" I could remember where I was and what I did, but as I looked for my brother in my memories of the violence, I could not see him in any of the scenes in my memory, even though I know he was there nearly all the time. I can recall us running to the telephone together. Suddenly, questions raced through my mind. "Where was he? Did he try to stop the fighting?" In my false sense of powerfulness, I always tried to stop the fighting, yelling from everything within me, "Don't hit my mama!" Did he yell, "Don't hit my mama," too? I could not recall him getting caught up in the chaos or fighting. I did not recall him ever yelling at my father. "Where was he? I know he was there. But, where was he?" Thinking about it, and not being able to recall the answer, I felt compelled to ask him.

Right away I called him on the telephone and we talked some, but I felt obligated to fly out to where he was and meet with him in person. He thought I was just being an overachiever and explained to me it was not necessary for us to meet face-to-face. We could do this over the telephone. To this day, I have a very close relationship with my brother. As kids we were like two peas in a pod. We were very close, always looking out for and parenting one another. I believe the trauma we experienced in childhood caused us to have a profound bond. I talk to my brother on a regular basis and can tell him my deepest secrets and scariest feelings. Our personalities are night and day different. My brother is a meek and humble man. For example, he can keep his mouth shut, whereas I have a difficult time not talking. If I have a thought, I think it needs to be shared with the world.

What I learned from our meeting was eye-opening. During the times we witnessed domestic violence, he was paralyzed by fear. He was so overwhelmed by what was taking place, he froze and stood still. He wanted to react, but could not respond or even move at times. When we were talking about our experiences and I got to the place where I asked him, "Where were you? I cannot see you in my mind." He broke down and cried and said, "I froze." From his tears and expression, I sensed he felt guilty for not fighting or speaking up or trying to intervene. Looking into his eyes, my mind flashed back to us as kids. Once again I saw the eyes of a little boy – eyes as large as saucers, body paralyzed by fear.

On that day, I hugged and held my brother as we sat in the restaurant and both cried. As we cried, I told him, "It was not your fault. You were just a little boy. You were not supposed to be placed in the position where you had to decide between you being hurt or watching Mom being abused." I was saying it to him and myself all at the same time. I went on to say, "It was too much for your brain to comprehend. It was too much for my brain to comprehend and make sense of. There is nothing for us to feel guilty or ashamed of." It was a freeing experience for me and for him. It was as if another layer of guilt and shame was lifted from our faces. In our conscious minds we knew we had been powerless to stop a monster. In our subconscious mind there was still a desire, a wish, that we could have saved and protected Mom from the abuse.

Lorenzo is a man of few words and little expression. As we finished up the conversation, he finally understood why I had traveled over 400 miles to meet with him. He said, "Now I know why you came. You could not have gotten this from a telephone conversation."

You or someone you know may have experienced something similar as a child. If so, I am saying the exact same thing to you. It is not your fault and it was not their fault. As children, we believed somehow or some way that we could have intervened or taken responsibility for an uncontrollable situation. You do not have to carry the guilt or shame of what happened; you were a witness. Your pain is real. It is pain that may be difficult to acknowledge or get in touch with. It may be hard to verbalize or comprehend because the scars are not on the surface. No one can see the emotional scars inflicted on the innocence of our souls. We can honor ourselves now by acknowledging our pain. Honor yourself by acknowledging the pain and give yourself permission to heal. If you need to weep, weep. You may even find a freedom in writing and expressing your feelings through journaling.

The more we talked, the more it was apparent his memories of witnessing domestic violence were in Technicolor. There were no fragmented memories for him. He remembers the night Mom was hospitalized in detail—nothing is hidden from his conscious mind.

He recalled how Mom ran into the room and grabbed us while our father was beating her. She tried to hold on to us while Dad was punching her and we were hit in the crossfire. I am sure Mom thought Dad would not hit her if she was holding on to us but that did not stop him. He was out of control and had crossed over into rage. He continued to punch her and us, but we did not receive the brunt of the punches. We were more terrorized than anything. In fact, we did not get checked out at the hospital, nor do I recall either of us having any scars or physical bruises. Our bruises were not physical, but mental and emotional. We carried invisible scars. As my brother shared how Mom held on to us, suddenly there was a flash across my mind—the little black box opened and released a bit of memory. The stage curtain lifted and I could remember Dad dragging Mom down the hallway to the back porch. The feelings of terror from this night are unforgettable. That night was, by far, the worst domestic violence episode we witnessed from our parents.

Our aunt and uncle arrived on the scene shortly after our call for help. Dad had locked the door and put the chain on so no one could get in.

They were on the outside of the door, attempting to kick the door in. My aunt was yelling at my Dad, "Mother f*#% open this damn door. Let us in. I'm going to kill you....You bastard, you better let us in mother f*#%." Bam, bam, bam! She yelled to us kids to open the door but Dad was shouting too, telling us to stay in our room and not to come out.

It felt like we were locked in our room. Invisible locks in our minds kept us in our room, from fear of our father's loud booming voice, fear of being beaten, and fear of Mom's death. Eventually, we snuck from our room and stood at the front door. "We can't open the door 'cause the chain is on," we yelled through the door.

When our aunt and uncle could not get in the front door, they ran around to the back door, and that's when they saw Mom. Our back porch was an open deck, so you could look down the street and see the whole neighborhood. From the ground there were about three or four flights of stairs before you reached our porch, but you could clearly see the platform of the balcony.

While our aunt and uncle were coming up the back stairs, Dad went out the front door and down the stairs. Dad had run downstairs so fast it sounded like he fell down. My brother described in detail how our father had hung our mother upside down like a piece of meat on the back porch with no clothes on. She was wrapped in cords of rope. He stood frozen at the kitchen counter as my aunt and uncle cut her down. I was there but wasn't there, deeply disassociated from the horror of the moment.

Another flash and the little black box opened again, lifting the curtain on a hidden memory. I saw myself leaning out the back door, gesturing frantically; I could not stand still. I was crying hysterically as my uncle and aunt took Mom down. Terror and panic gripped me. I wanted them to get her down; my sobbing was uncontrollable and I could hardly breathe. I looked at Mom and blood flowed from her nose and lips. Her eyes were swollen shut. She looked lifeless. I cried, "Please, please! Please help my mama!"

I was so focused on them getting Mom down and untied, that I did not know Dad had re-entered our apartment. He snatched up my brother and me, pulling us close to his chest and holding us tightly. With my brother and me in his arms, Dad carried us down the stairs. He held me in one arm and my brother in the other arm, as he had so many times before.

But this time it was different. He was angry. As I looked up at his eyes it was like looking into the eyes of a monster, but I knew the monster was my Dad. He was breathing hard, sweat dripping from his forehead. The wrinkles in his brow were protruding. As he was carrying us down the stairs, he said, "Do you guys want to go with me?"

We were terrified. We were caught in a dilemma, afraid to go with him and equally afraid to tell him "No." Saying "no" could cause Mr. Hyde to appear. If we said "no," he could hurt us. We knew that whatever Dad wanted, we did. We did everything we could to please him and make life easy for him, even at this young age. If he was happy, everybody was happy. We were frightened and scared to death of him, but somehow, somewhere, we mustered up the courage and shook our heads. "No, we don't want to go with you. We want to stay with Mom." This was the first time I can recall saying "no" to my father.

When we arrived downstairs, paramedics had just arrived. Two men took a gurney and ran toward the back of our building. Dad put us on the ground and said good-bye, then jumped into his car and sped off.

CHAPTER THREE
HOSPITALIZED

Abandoned on the curbside by our father, my brother and I stood watching as two men came towards us with Mom strapped down to a gurney. I was tormented by the thought Mom was dead or dying. At the age of five my biggest fear, which constantly plagued and preoccupied my mind, was that Dad was going to kill Mom.

I stood in the street and stared in fear and disbelief as the paramedics began to approach the ambulance. It felt as though they were moving in slow motion, yet it seemed as if everything else was magnified: horns were honking, people were talking, and cars were rolling down the street at an alarming speed. A few people had gathered on the sidewalk to see what was happening. Everyone else's life was going on as normal while I stood frozen in place, staring at the shiny door handles of the ambulance.

The ambulance doors appeared to be so cold. I was standing close to them, yet they seemed a million miles from me. They lifted the gurney and slid Mom into the ambulance. I wanted so desperately to go with her. Seeing those doors close had a terrible sense of finality about my Mom's life. Their closing boomed like thunder. The polished silver door handles locked shut, sounding like gun shots.

I thought for sure Mom's life was over. Her body seemed so lifeless—like my rag doll. I was familiar with death. We had a dog named Solomon that had gotten hit by a car and died. Mom's face, too, looked like she had been hit by a car. I was horrified by what I had seen when they wheeled her by us. Her facial disfigurement was so severe, she didn't even look human. She looked like a monster – a monster I could not bear to look at, yet a monster I wanted so desperately to see. The command center of my mind automatically opened and the terrible disfigurement of her face was placed in my black box.

Suddenly, the ambulance took off, rushing Mom to the hospital. Aunt Bertha was motioning for me to come to her. My feet felt like they had been planted in the street and I could not move them. I could see her gesturing for me to come to her. Her lips were moving as she called for me, but I couldn't hear the sound of her voice. The sounds around me had become muted, distorted by the sound of the ambulance doors slamming shut and locks ringing in my ears. Like a tape being played and rewound again and again, the ambulance was the only thing I could hear.

Time stood still. I was in shock.

Finally, Aunt Bertha realized I could not move, so she grabbed me and put me into their car while Walter helped my brother. Spell-broken, we both began to plead with them to take us to the hospital to see Mom. We were terrorized, worried and afraid for our Mom's life. We rushed to the hospital. The ambulance already had arrived at the hospital by the time we got there. We were not allowed to see her immediately. We had to sit in the waiting room. It was crowded and hot.

The memories of this night are forever crystallized in our minds for my brother and me. After talking with my brother, I was inspired to gather my mother and father's perspective on that terrible night. When I went to talk to both of them, I was surprised that they could only recall a few details from the grotesque episode. How could this be? When I queried Mom about the violence she endured that night, she said, "There was so much violence; I cannot even remember it all. Some things I choose to forget about and some things I just cannot recall."

The night Mom was hospitalized, I suspect Mom either disassociated or blacked out due to the trauma. In my heart's memory, I believe it happened as she was dragged down the hallway. Somewhere along the way she stopped fighting and resisting. Her body became as limp as a rag doll. In fact, she did not recall how she got to the hospital. She thought one of her sisters had taken her to the hospital, in contrast to that terrible memory I have of her being loaded into the ambulance and being rushed to the hospital.

Mom's most vivid memory from the night she was hospitalized is when she was lying on the gurney in the corridors of the hospital. She could hear voices and people walking by her, but she couldn't see anything.

Her face was so battered it was difficult to open her eyes. Focusing on the voices and sounds of conversation, she heard two women walking by and talking. As they saw her lying on the gurney, one woman said to the other, "That lady must have been hit by a truck or something." My Mom thought she recognized their voices. The other woman said, "Yeah," but then stopped suddenly. In a rush, she said, "Ma, that's Lil!" It was my Grandma Maeomia and Aunt Brenda. The hospital was so busy that night they could not get Mom into a room right away, and she was out in the hospital hallway waiting for a room assignment.

My father's memories are very scattered and he only vaguely recalls this evening. While he knows he was very violent that particular night, and remembers pushing his way into our apartment, he can recall only a few details. For him this night is like a black hole and extremely painful for him to attempt to remember what happened.

This particular night it was my Aunt Bertha and her fiancé Walter (he's my uncle now) who came to our rescue. They were both fresh out of high school when this occurred. Aunt Bertha and Walter were high school sweethearts and had become engaged while they were in high school. When I interviewed them, they recalled the night vividly. My Uncle Walter said what he remembered most was how traumatized my brother and I were when they arrived. He recalled how I was screaming and crying hysterically. This speaks to what I felt that night… nothing but terror. He also told of how badly my Mom was beaten and her being rushed to the hospital in an ambulance.

Aunt Bertha recalls how traumatic the night was, seeing her sister beaten beyond recognition. Mom was a beautiful young lady, a petite woman only 5'4" or less in height who weighed no more than 115 pounds. When my aunt saw the scars, bruises, and disfigurement of Mom's face, she was desperately afraid my Mom would never fully recover or look like herself again. They both recalled the horror of having to cut Mom down from where my father had hung her up on our back porch.

It is only by the grace of God that Mom lived through this event without any facial scarring or permanent damage to her brain. The doctors were concerned Mom was going to have some type of brain damage due to her injuries and hanging upside down. Once she was placed in a room, my brother and I were allowed to see her and know for ourselves that our worst fear had not come true; she was still alive. I remember walking into her hospital room.

Grandma Maeomia and Aunt Brenda were standing at Mom's bedside. Barely able to open her eyes, Mom heard us enter the room and as best she could, began to raise her head and turn away from us. She cried out, "Don't let my kids see me. Please don't let them see me like this." As quickly as we had walked in, we were ushered out of the room.

Nothing else was said to us about that night. What we saw, what we heard, what we thought and felt was never addressed.

Throughout the years of violence, neighbors never came to our rescue. Everyone seemed to think they just needed to mind their own business. Not this time or any other time was there ever any outside intervention beyond family members.

CHAPTER FOUR
BELIEVING THE LIE

After the incident when Mom was hospitalized, Dad went into hiding. It was scary not knowing where he was at. From the time Dad left us on the sidewalk, he did not call us or anything. I worried about him and missed him, too. We stayed with Grandma Maeomia for a number of days where it was safe. I felt confused. While I missed Dad, at the same time I felt like I had to really stay on guard, not knowing when or where he would show up.

Eventually we went back to our same apartment. Every day I looked for him to come. Most of the time when he returned it was in the evening with a gentle knock at the door. He was nice then. The majority of the times before he would return, his mother, Grandma Kathleen, would come over and talk to Mom. I could never sit in the living room and listen to their conversations. Lorenzo and I were ushered off to play in our room or in the back playroom. I never could hear what was being said, but I would play with one eye on my toys and the other eye watching Mom.

They would sit and talk for what seemed like hours. When my grandma Kathleen arrived it would be daylight and by the time she left it would be dark outside. I can remember seeing my mother's face by the end of the conversations. Her eyes would be puffed up and red from crying. I do not recall my grandma Kathleen showing much emotion or affection. She seemed rather motionless and unemotional about the situation. She was a woman of few words and mainly listened. I would imagine she was a type of negotiator. Dad would send either her or someone else over before he would reappear. This was his way of testing the waters.

Days and weeks went by with no word from Dad. The next thing we knew, he had moved to Minneapolis, Minnesota and landed a really good job as a city bus driver. My Uncle Charles, who was also living in Minneapolis, came to our apartment and spoke with my mother. They talked in the living room.

My Uncle Charles was tall, brown-skinned, and handsome. His skin color had a red hue to it. He always appeared well-dressed and well-groomed. He was more educated and articulate than my father.

During those times when my grandma Kathleen would come over, I felt more at ease. Having my Uncle Charles there was different. I did not trust Uncle Charles. Looking into his eyes, I feared there was a monster inside of him, too. I was afraid he would become violent like my Dad. Even more so than usual, I stayed alert as they talked. I felt so anxious about Charles being there, I had to walk into the living room every now and then to ask a question. I had to know what was going on, and what he was saying. Plus, I needed to check on Mom and make sure she was okay. Watching Mom, her faced looked puzzled as she listened intently. She cried some, but not like she cried with Grandma Kathleen. There was also relief on her face. She finally knew where my father was and he was miles away. I could tell she really wanted to believe my uncle and was looking for a ray of hope.

Uncle Charles reported that my father was working, saving money and changing. Looking deeper into my uncle's eyes, I could see he was smiling on the inside. To me it felt like he was a devil in disguise. He could see he was winning her over. I recall walking out of the room, staring hard at him, and wishing he would go away. Mom was so naïve; she thought my uncle was truthful, honest, and a good person. She believed the lie. She was desperate and willing to do anything to have our family restored.

The meeting with my Uncle Charles was the beginning of Dad working his way back into our family. It wasn't long before Dad made his way back into our lives. The gifts started to come. Mom received diamond earrings and clothes, and we got lots of gifts that Christmas. I remember the day we came home and bunk beds were set up in our bedroom. Mom was so excited—she had always wanted bunk beds for us. She had the biggest smile on her face when she showed them to us.

The beds were wrapped in plastic and brand new. We had never had brand new beds before. Lorenzo was thrilled with the new beds. He slept on the top and I slept on the bottom bunk. One time Lorenzo fell out of the top bunk bed. He didn't hurt himself too badly, as there were no broken bones or bruises. We began sharing the bottom bunk until Dad could put guard rails up for us.

The new beds gave us more space in our bedroom. I loved the bunk beds, but mostly I was excited because they made Mom happy. Up until that point, I don't remember my father spending much money or time with us.

Then one day Dad appeared again. He acted as if he had never left. It was like he had been with us all the time and never really left. Of course, he came bearing gifts for us all. I received another doll. Lorenzo received more G.I. Joe toys. We were both so happy to see Dad. After all, he was still our father. Dad held me in one arm and Lorenzo in the other. Dad squeezed us so tight and told us how much he loved us until we burst out in laughter and giggles.

It seemed like everything was back to normal after Dad's visit. We were back together as a family. Dad continued to live in Minneapolis and visited us on a number of occasions. Once we went to see him in Minneapolis. Lorenzo and I actually got to fly on an airplane for the first time in our lives. Mom went with us, too. We had a lot of fun. We played outside in snow, built snowmen, made angels, and went tobogganing.

Weeks later, without a whole lot of notice, Mom announced we were moving to Minneapolis to be a family again. I was happy to have Dad back in our lives. He played with us more and spent time with us. With his smile, laughter and hugs, he lit up my world. Looking into his eyes, it seemed as if the monster had disappeared. Things were better now. We were ready to move forward.

Even though the times were good and the monster seemed like he had left, still I remained on guard sleeping with one eye open, always ready to defend Mom.

It was not very long from the time Mom made the announcement we were moving that we started packing things up. Dad got a big moving truck so we could move all our furniture. With the help of Uncle Charles and some of Dad's other friends, they loaded all of our things onto the moving truck and we were Minneapolis bound. Before we left Chicago, Mom stopped by our school to get our records. She explained to the office administrators we were moving and would finish the school year in Minneapolis.

As we drove away from Chicago, and I watched the huge skyscrapers of downtown Chicago become like toy buildings in the distance, I had mixed emotions. Minneapolis was a long way away from Chicago. The drive took forever. I kept asking if we were there yet. It was not long before I glanced back, and there was no sign of Chicago, or Grandma Maeomia, my aunts, or those we could call for help if we needed it. For the first time in my life, we were on our own.

From the backseat, I could see Dad's eyes through the rearview mirror. His eyes looked straight ahead, occasionally turning to look at my Mom. There was no sign of the monster.

The excitement of moving to a new place with my Mom and Dad soon outweighed some of the uneasiness I felt. Dad stopped along the way as much as he could. Uncle Charles drove the truck as we rode in Mom's bright yellow 1972 Ford Mustang. Dad and Uncle Charles switched back and forth between driving the moving truck and Mom's car. When we stopped, Dad bought us hamburgers, fries, and milkshakes. He'd also picked up some candy bars to snack on during the ride. Grandma Maeomia had sent fried chicken, homemade biscuits, apples, and oranges for our long journey. When we arrived in Minneapolis, we were stuffed, but exhausted.

My Dad's apartment was nice, but not as big as the one we had in Chicago. It only had one bedroom, so our bunk beds were set up in a large open space, probably intended for a dining room.

I was thrilled to be close to my parents' bedroom. With this arrangement, I could always listen to what was happening in the kitchen or their bedroom. We settled into our new apartment in Minneapolis, and I felt some sense of relief. Finally, my Mom and Dad were back together again and living under the same roof. I was so happy because I loved both of my parents and had longed for them to be back together. Even though I was fearful of my father, I wanted so desperately for him to be with us.

We were not in Minneapolis very long before the arguing started. Arguing led to fighting. Dad would yell and turn his music up loud to drown out the yelling. Suddenly I would hear SMACK! The next sound was Mom crying. In Minneapolis, it seemed most of the fighting usually took place behind closed doors. It was not the outburst of rage or severe fighting I had witnessed in the past. I was always attentive to the sounds of what was around us. At nighttime I would lie on my back in the bed and just listen to what was going on. At times things were pleasant. Mom and Dad seemed to be having a good time playing, laughing, and listening to music. Then there were other times I could feel anger and rage in the atmosphere. During those times I would lie in the bed silently, staying very still so I could listen even more closely, hoping I would not have to take action. I would keep my eyes open, fighting to stay awake as long as possible. But if Dad came in the room, I would quickly shut my eyes, pretending to be asleep.

During those times, hearing Dad yell sent chills down my spine, but no one ever knew it. I would use my imagination and pretend like I was not afraid. Showing fear was a sign of weakness and I knew I could not be weak. I had to be strong and a fighter, for Mom's sake. When Dad would yell his voice sounded like thunder and it felt like the whole world could hear him. His yelling was frightening but hearing or seeing Mom getting hit made me even more fearful. It was a different kind of fear, though. It was a fear which fueled and provoked my own anger and rage. Fear became like gasoline to the flames of my anger. I never knew what was going to happen next. And, who could we call? How could we stop the monster?

Once the fighting and yelling subsided, Mom would leave their bedroom, heading to the bathroom or to the kitchen. I would check her face for scars, bumps, bruises, or some sort of disfigurement. To my surprise, I did not see the bruises I had seen in the past. Then, looking deeply into her eyes (which was so painful to do), I could see she was silently crying and screaming for help. She was hurting so badly, yet she was locked up inside. In her eyes there was a hopelessness that had not been there before.

Mom was a positive person, always finding a way to get things done and make things happen. Whatever we wanted, she found a way to get it for us; it was just a matter of time. She would explain: "I do not have the money right now, but we will save up for it and get it later." Later always came. Mom consistently delivered on her promises. Whatever she said, I knew I could count on it. Looking into her eyes, I could see she was changing. The abuse had begun to take a toll on her like never before. Even when she was smiling it seemed like she was frowning. I worried about her constantly and would often ask, "Are you okay? What's wrong, Mom?" She never would tell me. We did not have an outlet to call for help. The support system we had relied heavily upon in the past was miles away.

As time went on, the arguing and fighting became more frequent and grew worse. Dad's thunderous voice was becoming even louder. Mom smiled less and cried more. Then it happened—for the last time. I was lying in my bed listening to them argue, with eyes wide open, keeping my body very still. I needed to hear everything and not be distracted by the sounds of my own movement. My brother was sleeping on the other side of the room. He had already fallen asleep. My eyes were heavy, but I knew I had to stay awake. I had to stay on guard. I could not call Grandma, aunts or uncles anymore. They were too far away. Dad had his music playing very loudly, but you could hear the boom in his voice over the music.

Suddenly, I heard their bedroom door crash open. There was a scuffle. Mom was trying to break free. My heart stop beating and I could feel my voice drop deep into the pit of my stomach. I felt like a lion getting ready to roar. I rose up from my pillow. I did not even make it out of my bed before I saw them, Mom running as fast as she could and Dad close behind with one arm extended, reaching out for her, trying to pull her back into the prison of their bedroom. He could confine and restrain her there.

It seemed everything was in slow motion: Dad reaching out to grab Mom and snatch her back, and the terror in Mom's eyes. I had seen this look on her face so many times before. Looking at Dad, he was no longer himself. The monster had returned. As they turned the corner for my bed, I could feel Mom's desperation and fear. She reached out for me, screaming for help, "Nissi, he's going to hit me." I can still sense the rage and intensity in the atmosphere. What really scared me was that my own demons were surfacing.

The demons of anger, rage, and indignation superseded all my fears. Looking Dad straight in the eye, I yelled with the roar of a lion, "DON'T HIT MY MAMA!" It all happened so fast I never even got out of bed to stand up, but I felt my body seething with rage. I was afraid but I wasn't afraid. It seemed I had my own demonic host which resided inside of me. I was six years old when this happened. I have never been able to escape or forget this night. It would be the last time I shouted this to my Dad.

Spell-broken, Dad stopped in his tracks and looked puzzled as Mom clung to me. Then, as if he was awakened from a trance, he turned around without saying a word. Dad returned to his bedroom and closed the door. He turned his music off and went to bed.

Mom was shaking and crying as she crawled into bed with me that night. We never talked about it. She did not say anything to me about what happened until I started writing this book. We slept together that night, holding each other. This was the last time I had to ward off the monster on Mom's behalf. It was one of the few times that I felt the demonic host of rage overtake me.

It was obvious Mom no longer believed the lie that things were going to be better. Just a day or two later our lives as we knew it would change forever.

Chapter Five
The Day Everything Changed

The monster, long absent from my Dad's eyes, was back that night. I was frightened like never before. I could tell from the way Mom held on to me that night, that she was more fearful than I was. When she ran to my bed, she was not just running to get away. The look of desperation in her eyes said she was running for her life. It was different this time—we had no place to hide. When we lived in Chicago, we could go and stay with Grandma Maeomia for a number of days. For some reason, Dad would never come get us from there. Now there was no one to help us and not a safe person to whom we could turn.

The next day things seemed to be back to normal. Mom slept in the room with Dad. I felt a little safer because Dad was not yelling, but I still was on alert and keeping my eyes open wide, staying awake as long as I could at night and listening carefully to the sounds around me. Our kitchen faucet leaked. It had a sound like drip, drop, constantly. At times the constant dripping of the sink was like music to my ears, because if I could hear the constant dripping that meant everything else was quiet—no loud music, no yelling, no screaming, and no fighting.

A few days went by and everything was normal. Sometimes Dad worked a split shift so he would leave early in the morning and then return early afternoon to go back to work late afternoon. Other days Dad worked an evening shift, so we would stay home all day with him. During the work week, Mom would wake my brother and me. She would have us get dressed and then feed us breakfast. If Dad wasn't home that day, then all three of us would leave the apartment. Our schedule varied. One thing that was consistent though was Mom always worked the same shift and left for work at the same time. She always left in the morning, generally catching the city bus to work.

This day was anything but typical. This was the day everything changed, forever. This morning, Mom did not get us up but rather let us wake up on our own. My brother was a sleeper, so he lingered in bed as usual. Sometimes he would tarry so long in getting dressed that Mom and I would dress him while he was still sleeping.

I remember waking up to the sound of things being scurried around in the long hallway closet next to our bedroom. It was a homemade closet with a long metal pole hanging between two chains suspended from the ceiling. This was where my parents hung most of their clothes.

I got out of bed and looked around the corner to see what was making all the noise. Mom was on her knees in the closet and her feet were sticking out. I went to the bathroom. When I came out, I noticed Mom was not dressed for work. She was not wearing her usual pretty suit or dress. She still had on her pajamas. By this time she was sitting on the floor of the closet looking at some of her old clothes, reminiscing. She had pulled out her orange suit and held it close to her. It was one of Mom's favorite outfits. Tears welled in her eyes as she held tightly to the fabric.

I thought to myself, What's wrong with her? Doesn't she need to get ready for work?" Next I thought, "maybe it's the weekend and she does not have to go to work," but it didn't seem like the weekend. In a rush of anxiety, I asked her, "Do we need to start getting dressed? Are you going to work today? Is it the weekend?" Mom slowly turned to face me with love in her eyes and said, "Not today. I'm not going to work today."

I asked, "What are you doing?" She responded, "Just getting some things out of the closet." I replied with an "okay," went back into my bedroom and started playing with some of my dolls. My brother woke up and I told him Mom was not going to work and we could stay home. He smirked as he rolled over to put his pillow over his head and go back to sleep. I continued to play with my dolls on the floor.

Mom periodically walked by, carrying clothes from the hallway closet and moving them into their bedroom. I finished playing with my dolls and got dressed for the day. By the time I was dressed, Mom had made her way into the kitchen and started making our favorite breakfast, French toast. Sometimes she allowed me to make the French toast by myself. She would push a chair up to the stove, and I would stand on the chair and watch it as it cooked. When I thought it was finished cooking on one side, I turned the French toast over with a spatula all by myself. Mom taught me I could do anything, and she would let me try almost anything.

My brother got dressed and we played all day with our toys in our room. Mom continued to move clothes from the closet to the bedroom in a slow, methodical fashion. It seemed with every step she took, the weight of the world was on her shoulders. When she was not in the closet moving clothes around, she was in her bedroom with the door closed.

We had lunch. Then Mom ran her bath water and finally got dressed. She just was not herself. Looking into her eyes, I could see her heart was broken. There was a deep sense of hopelessness and despair in the atmosphere. It was a nice, sunny, warm summer day in Minneapolis, but watching Mom it felt like it was raining all over the world.

We were playing in our room when Mom walked in and said she needed to talk to us. Both Lorenzo and I put down our toys and looked at her. Her shoulders were slumped. With a look of dismay she stared at the floor. We all sat together on my bed. She explained to us she was leaving. She said, "Your Dad and I are not getting along. I am afraid of what could happen to him or me. I do not have a place for us all to go to, so I am going to leave and find a place for us. Once I find a place for us to live, I will come back and get you two."

My heart dropped to the pit of my stomach. "Leave… us… Mom is going to leave us." There was a loud ringing in my ears. I could hear her saying, "…but I will come back for you two." The dripping sound from the kitchen faucet which had comforted me at night was completely gone. I couldn't hear any other sound except, "I am coming back for you two." I gasped for air and wanted to cry but I would not, could not let Mom see me cry. As much as it pained me to hear it, there was part of me that knew and understood she needed to leave. At the same time, I did not want her to leave without us. The other night I had seen the demon reappear. I had already been fretting in my mind this reappearance and how would I respond. I dreaded another confrontation. What if the demon got out of control again?

Suddenly, I heard my conscious mind shouting to my subconscious mind. "Emergency! Emergency! Sound the alarm. I must request access to the black box." Sirens were going off in my mind and my senses were on alert. I could feel the tears beginning to well up in my eyes, but I fought them back. My conscious mind was saying, "Don't shed a tear… don't shed a tear." The black box was opened and access was given. The keeper of the black box waited in high anticipation as my conscious mind debated with my subconscious mind. I could hear them haggling back and forth… "What would you like to deposit? Where is the deposit? Do you have it?"

All of a sudden the black box was open. Deposits were being made into the black box…. "Don't cry; don't say anything. Don't tell her how you really feel. You'll make it too hard for her to leave. You've got to let her go now. This is the only way. Don't cry… she is leaving Dad." As suddenly as the box was opened, it was immediately shut with new messages inside. My conscious mind was abruptly ushered back into our bedroom. There we were sitting on the bed with Mom explaining to us that she was leaving.

No tears fell from my eyes that day. Mom never knew I wanted to cry. I felt numb all over. My eyes focused on the carpet floor and I searched in my mind for the sound of the constant dripping of the kitchen faucet. As I regained my consciousness, I gazed over at my brother searching for a trace of a tear in his eyes or a track of tears on his face. Nothing was there. No tears. His eyes were glazed over, and there was a look of hopelessness and despair. Looking into Mom's eyes, there was deep fear and a void. Physically she was still with us, but mentally and emotionally she was already gone. A mere shell of who she was stood before us. All of her hope had evaporated; she was exhausted. When Mom finished talking, we did not argue or even attempt to discourage her from leaving. Without further explanation or discussion, my brother and I both understood the cost associated with Mom staying. We simply said "okay" and that was it. In our hearts we were willing to be left behind and would have done ANYTHING to know she was safe.

A few moments later, Mom walked into her bedroom and emerged with two suitcases. Once they were loaded into her car, she came back to say goodbye. She hugged us so tight, but it was hard to feel her hug. My body had gone numb again. I was fighting to feel my legs. The black box was cracked open again, and a deposit was made. My imagination attempted to overpower my conscious mind and disputed reality. My imagination was adamantly indicating, "This really isn't happening. It is all a bad dream. She is leaving Dad, not you."

I smiled at Mom as she stepped back to walk out the door. I smiled as if I were a circus clown distracting a lion from eating his master. I looked at my brother and he was smiling, too. He, too, was a circus clown that was smiling on the outside but fearful, sad and crying on the inside. As she got ready to walk away, she handed me a cassette tape and said, "Give this tape to your Dad when he gets home." I looked at the cassette tape and was puzzled by it. Then she closed and locked the back door. I could hear her footsteps as she walked down the stairs to her bright yellow Mustang, leaving us behind.

The car door slowly opened, luggage was loaded, and then the door closed. She sat in the parking lot for what seemed a long time. I could feel her eyes looking up at us even though we could not see her. I knew she was contemplating if this was the right decision. In my heart I sent her a message, "You must go now." The engine roared as she started the car, and the sound gradually decreased as she drove away. All at once, without uttering a word, my brother and I looked at each other. We ran to the window to see if we could see Mom driving down the street. My brother spotted her first. "There she is!" he yelled.

We stood at the window until her car was no longer in sight. As Mom's bright yellow Mustang faded out of sight, I could hear the constant dripping of the kitchen faucet again. A deep sense of loneliness filled my heart, replacing the numbness. Then a sense of relief flooded my heart so powerfully it drowned out all my loneliness. Looking at my brother, I could tell he felt a powerful sense of relief, too. Mom would not have to face the monster again. After watching cars go by for several minutes, we stepped away from the window and returned to our bedroom. Neither of us said anything.

As I was walking back to the bedroom, I looked at the cassette tape and wondered what was on it. I felt a sense of pride thinking about how Mom had entrusted me with the cassette tape. Even though I was not the oldest, I acted, felt, and pretended like I was older than my brother. I loved being responsible and to have Mom to depend on me. As I looked at the cassette tape, I suddenly understood. Mom had the tape recorder with her all day and had made a cassette tape with her talking, although I did not hear what she had said.

My mind flashed back to us sitting on the bed and Mom explaining, "Your Dad and I are not getting along." The black box was gently opened and a message was put inside again…. "Mom is leaving Dad." Slowly the black box was closed as I stared at the cassette tape for a few more moments. Then I placed it softly on the dresser. I climbed into my bed and lay still for a while staring at the ceiling, listening to the kitchen faucet drip and wondering when Mom would return for us. Listening attentively, I waited to hear Dad put his key in the front door but there was no sound. I waited and waited, then slowly eased out of my bed onto the floor to play with my dolls. Suddenly, I could hear footsteps and keys. The key was going into the key chamber at the front door. "Oh," I thought to myself, "maybe she is coming back for us. Mom must have changed her mind about leaving us." I jumped to my feet and ran to the door.

The door swung wide open. My heart soared with hope, then dropped with disappointment when I saw it was just Dad, home from work. He looked at me and said "Hey, Princess." My eyes fell to the carpet floor and I responded with a quiet, "Hi." I followed a little ways behind him as he walked back to their bedroom, removing his tie as he went. He quickly came out saying, "Where's your Mom?"

"She left," I answered.

"Where did she go?"

"I don't know," I told him. "She left you a cassette tape."

We walked to my bedroom and I gave him the cassette tape I had laid on the dresser. He looked at me perplexed and confused, then he focused his eyes on the cassette tape as he walked back to his bedroom to listen to it. At first, his door was open and I could hear it was Mom's voice on the cassette tape. Then he abruptly closed the door. I wondered what was on the cassette tape, but was too afraid to ask if I could listen. I could hear Mom's voice, but could not make out what she was saying. I returned to my dolls on the floor and combed their hair.

Suddenly the bedroom door was flung open and Dad's thunderous voice boomed out, calling me, "Nissi, Nissi!" I jumped to my feet and started towards his room. Before I could even get out of my room, he was there filling the doorway and looking larger than life. His face was red and I could see a look of growing hysteria. Panicked, he shouted at me, "Where did she go?" I could see the same terror in his eyes that I had felt so many times. It was the terror of not knowing how you are going to survive, the place where you begin to question your own existence. It is where you question if you have the ability to overcome your current situation. It is the place where you know things will never be the same again.

Hoping I could calm him down, I looked down at the carpet floor and responded softly without making eye contact. Hands clasped behind my back, I shook my head side to side and I said, "I don't know where she went." When I looked up, his eyes had begun to well with tears. His voice became soft and childlike as tears begin to stream down his face. "I have got to find her and bring her back," he said. "She can't leave you guys with me. I can't take care of you. I don't know how to take care of you. I can't do this."

I searched for words to comfort him. He was no longer larger than life. My mind raced as I saw the demon was no longer powerful, but a powerless and defeated foe. I focused my eyes intently on him. Softly, I said, "She's coming back for us. She's going to find a place to live and come back for us." Instead of these words comforting Dad, they were like fuel to a fire. Instantly, he became more hysterical and intense. Like turning a light switch on, suddenly the monster was back and I was afraid. Roaring with anger, resentment and rage, he said, "I'm going to go find her and bring her back."

My knees weakened and I was terrified. My conscious mind sent the message…. "Maybe this time he will hurt you." Immediately the black box reopened and sirens were going off in my mind. My subconscious mind took the reins. It shouted "NO FEAR!!! NO FEAR HERE!!!" A message was placed in the black box. "Don't be afraid. You are not afraid. Don't ever let him or anyone know when you feel scared. Stand still. Hold your ground. You can't run and hide. No time for hiding. No time for running. No fear here."

Then the interrogation began. He had a thousand questions. "What was she wearing? What time did she leave? Which way did she go?" Dad then hurried us into the kitchen and placed us in front of the stove. There was a clock on the stove which I had never noticed before. He stood both my brother and I in front of it and questioned us as to where the big hand and little hand were when Mom had left. I was too afraid to look at my brother because I could feel his fear. I was always the spokesperson for us. Neither of us had looked at the clock to see what time it was when she had left. The pressure was overwhelming; neither of us knew how to tell time or concerned ourselves with the clock. Desperately, I tried to think of something to say. My brother was very quiet. The wrong answer could potentially provoke a violent response. Both Dad and Mom taught us to never lie. Our punishments were always much worse if we lied. Mom said our nose would grow like Pinocchio's.

My palms started to perspire, then my face began to feel very warm and eventually I could feel the sweat beading on the top my head. It seemed like we stood in front of the clock for hours with Dad asking the same questions over and over again, "Where was the big hand, where was the little hand?" We kept shaking our heads side to side, repeating ourselves, "I don't know. We didn't look at the clock. We can't tell time." When we could not give him any information, he became angrier and angrier. With a roar in his voice he bent over and leaned into us, pointing with his finger and said, "If you knew what time she left or what direction she went, I could find her."

My conscious mind and subconscious mind began to wage war against each other as they fought for position for placing messages into the black box. The black box was opened and my conscious mind logged the following entries:

> "Time is real important."
> "Pay close attention to time."
> "I wish I knew how to tell time."
> "You better learn how to tell time soon."

My subconscious mind logged:

> "It's a good thing you don't know how to tell time."
> "Not knowing how to tell time helped Mom to get away."
> "Time is only important to the monster."
> "It's not your fault."
> "She didn't leave you; she left him."

The black box was closed.

Finally, Dad left the apartment with only a curt message, "I will be back." He went looking for Mom, but he never found her that day. When he returned, we had a very quiet dinner. Mom did not call and we did not know where she was. I did not feel like playing with my toys anymore that night, so I put my pajamas on and climbed into the bed. I lay there and stared at the ceiling, feeling a small sense of comfort knowing Mom had gotten away and she would come back for us soon. There was no yelling, no screaming, and no fighting that night.

Just a few days after Mom had left us, Dad took a picture of Lorenzo and I (see end of chapter). Dad was planning on getting it to Mom in hopes, when she saw us, she would return. I remember the day we took the picture; it was a difficult day. My brother and I dressed ourselves. After I had gotten dressed I looked in the mirror and realized my hair was a complete mess. It had not been combed since Mom had left. I went to Dad with tears in my eyes and said, "What about my hair? I can't take a picture or go outside like this."

Neither Dad nor I knew how to comb my hair. Dad suggested I wear a scarf on my head and take the picture. I never had worn a scarf before. Mom always kept me well groomed and presentable. I felt so ashamed and deeply abandoned that Mom was not there to care for me or my hair. The black box was opened once again and deposits were made: "You have to learn how to take care of yourself. No one will really take care of you. Don't depend on other people; they will let you down." As suddenly as the black box was opened, it was slammed shut.

As we stood there, I began to dream of what it was going to be like when Mom returned for us. I missed her so much that it was difficult to smile. I felt a deep sense of despair and loneliness without her. I was torn between two worlds. On one hand I was elated she was gone, because it meant Dad could not hurt her anymore. Yet, I was devastated that Mom had not returned for us. I didn't think it was going to take so long for her to come back for us.

Abruptly, my mind was ushered back into the room with Dad. He was standing in front of my brother and me with the camera and saying, "Smile for your mama." My heart was completely broken inside and all I wanted to do was cry. As we were standing there, I could see my brother was crying on the inside, too. But, somehow, someway, we managed to muster up our circus clown smiles so Dad could take the picture. I was six years old and my brother was eight.

She walked away and it set me free

No longer did fear and worry have a hold on me.

I became free to be me.

Fighting to be something more than me.

It set me free to be me.

The anxiety and stress of setting her free no longer had its claim on me.

It was tormenting to see things I shouldn't see.

It was tormenting to me to see the chains which clung to me.

I was not free but life had bonded and branded me.

Yes, branded by things I did not want to see.

Bonded by a love that was confusing me.

Chaos and insanity was constantly tormenting me.

Where was my protector?

Who will stand up for me?

I so desire to be set free.

I so desire to be me.

Please walk away.

Oh, how I don't want you to live or end life this way.

It's a horrible, horrible, state; oh please hurry before it is too late.

Oh, please don't stay in this state; if you wait it might be too late.

You must go now. You must walk away to be free.

And, then torment, anxiety and fear will no longer have a hold on me.

CHAPTER SIX
A PLAN DEVISED

"I'm going to come back for you...."

Mom's promise played over and over in my head like a broken record. I tried to forget how her voice trembled under the weight of her emotions. I tried to forget how she cried. Mom's tear-filled eyes the day she left was a memory stored in the black box. Yet, I held tightly to the promise of her return. Sometimes at night, while lying in bed, I felt Mom's kiss upon my forehead. I heard her tender voice. Her voice would say, "I love you, Nissi." I felt her presence.

The days following after Mom had left were grueling. Seeing unending fear, anxiety, and worry in Dad's eyes was painful. It seemed like the sun had stopped shining and the sky was filled with dark clouds. The monster had not disappeared but seemed to be camouflaged. Dad walked around in a state of confusion. He seemed to move in slow motion. As each day went by, the light in his eyes grew dimmer and his skin darkened. Loneliness filled the atmosphere. It was obvious he missed Mom and was devastated by her leaving. My brother and I missed her, too. In my heart, I could feel she was safe and looking for a place for us to live. Everything was quiet except for the constant dripping of the kitchen faucet. Lying in bed at night, the dripping faucet was the only sound I would hear. It seemed louder than it had been before and now had become annoying.

A few days went by without any word from Mom. Dad was becoming more worried and irritated. He was trying to do everything he could to find her and would have done anything to have her back. As each day went by my brother and I worked harder in an attempt to please Dad. He was like a wild lion which had been tamed by the cage of circumstances. We did whatever we could to keep him calm and make things easier for him. We dressed ourselves and ate lots of peanut butter and jelly sandwiches.

In the evening after dinner my brother and I would push our chairs up to the kitchen sink to do the dishes. I would stand on the chair at the kitchen sink as close to the door as possible, so I could wash dishes, keep an eye on Dad's bedroom door and hear what he was saying. I worried about him and was not sure what he was going to do next. Sometimes I would hear him crying, which made my heart feel heavy. He sounded like a lion which had a thorn in his paw. I wanted to run and rescue him but was too fearful and it was dangerous to approach a lion.

It was painful to see and hear him cry. It was also confusing to witness how hard Dad was taking Mom's departure. One moment he was sad and depressed. The next moment he seemed to be very angry about his predicament. He never thought she would leave, especially without us. Looking deep into his eyes it was apparent the monster had not left, but depending on the day or circumstances, wore a different mask. Sometimes the monster even seemed to be subdued. During those times Dad was unresponsive and did not show any emotions. You never knew when the monster was going to reappear in full force. The monster could show up without notice so I had to watch for him all the time.

As a number of days went by, Dad started to panic. Denial was wearing off and the reality of Mom's departure started to set in. Mom had never left us with him or with anyone. He began to realize Mom was serious this time. It was evident she had no intention of coming back to him. As the days dragged on, terror finally gripped Dad. He started frantically making telephone calls to family members and friends, explaining that Mom had left. He was also seeking advice on what to do. I would hear him over and over fearfully saying, "I cannot take care of these kids; she's supposed to come back for them."

He finally spoke with my grandmother, who gave him the good news. Mom was safe. We did not know where she was, but we knew she was safe. We were all thrilled to hear the good news. Dad was pleased and annoyed at the same time. From the time Mom left, Dad wanted to keep us close by him and was paranoid. When he went to work he took us with him. He was a city bus driver, so we rode with him on his bus route. It was so much fun to go to work with him. When he had a break in his route he let us put on his bus driver's hat and sit at the bus wheel. The steering wheel was so big and Dad let us play with it. But we could not touch the pedals or any of the big red, blue, or yellow buttons. When we came home we had to stay in the house and play in our room.

Then it finally happened. Dad said it was okay for us to go outside. I was elated! In my heart I had expected if we were outside playing, Mom would see us and pick us up. When Dad said we could go outside, I got dressed as fast as I could. My heart begin to pound faster and faster as I anticipated being in Mom's presence. I ran down the back stairs where Mom's car was usually parked. It was early morning so no other kids were outside. My heartbeat subsided as I stood outside frozen by disappointment. Looking around in search of Mom's car, I was dismayed by disbelief. How could it be? She was not there.

Outwardly, no tears fell from my eyes on that day. Inwardly, there was a river of tears that welled up inside of me and wanted to flow from my eyes and roll down my cheeks. As I cried on the inside, I stood there. My heart became heavier as I fought back tears and negative thoughts which attempted to ravage my mind. My legs weakened and vision blurred as I stared at two cars in the parking lot.

The black box was opened and memories of the day Mom left were crystal clear. Within myself I said, "She has got to be here. Her car has to appear... she has got to be here. She promised me." In my head I could hear her saying over and over, "I am going to come back for you." I focused my mind on thoughts of her return. In an attempt to drown out all my fears, I let her statement ring loudly in my heart and mind. Then I began to say within myself, "She's coming back for you." As tears continued to well up inside me, I muttered those words over and over. "She's coming back." The black box closed.

As the days went by I continued to tell myself daily, "She's coming back for you," and repeated my routine of looking for Mom in the parking lot, on every corner, and at the community center. Each morning I would awaken and spring out of bed with one prevailing thought on my mind: "Today might be the day Mom comes back for us." Each night I went to bed with mixed emotions. I was disappointed she had not come back for us, yet on the other hand, I was relieved Dad was not beating her. At night I lay in bed staring at the ceiling, listening to the kitchen faucet and imagining Mom's return for us.

A few weeks went by and Dad was getting worse. His smile had totally dissipated. You could see stress marks in his forehead. Tear tracks and frown lines on his face became more apparent. He would almost run to his bedroom when he got home from work, so he could be alone and make telephone calls. He had a difficult time looking at us. He was stressed by all the responsibility that came with being a single parent. The roles had been reversed. Dad was afraid Mom was going to come back for us and he would be left all alone. The thought of her coming back for us seemed to torment him and caused the monster to manifest itself in different forms like deep discontentment, anger, and depression. Dad wanted so desperately for Mom to return and would have done anything within his power to influence her to come back.

As time went on, there was a shift from telephone conversations to visits. Uncle Charles and other close friends would come to visit with Dad. Dad was seeking advice, strategizing, and planning. The consensus was that the key to my Mom's return was us. I would overhear a number of our family members and Dad's friends saying, "She wants those kids. I bet if you keep those kids from her, she will come back to you. She can't live without them kids. Don't let her have those kids. Don't even let her talk to those kids and she will run back to you." That's when a plan was devised.

One evening, Dad came home from work and without any notice began to pack some of our clothes. He eventually told us we were going to Maplewood, Minnesota, a small city about forty minutes from Minneapolis, to spend the weekend with Tia. Tia was my Uncle Charles's girlfriend and mother of two of his children. Tia had a total of six children, four older and two younger. It felt like my heart dropped and fell to the floor in a million pieces at the news of us leaving our apartment. Fear and anxiety began to grip my throat and I could hardly breathe. I thought about Tia's six kids and their huge German Sheppard dog named Shaft. Tia's house was chaotic, confusing, and dysfunctional. Kids ran the house because Tia was never home. We had visited Tia's home a number of times but, for me, our visits could not have been short enough. Then it dawned on me. "If we weren't at home, how could Mom pick us up?"

Dad's words were law. No appeal was allowed..

There was no time to ask him questions or voice concerns that day. Dad loaded several of our things into the car and dragged us out the door. As we drove off, I looked back at our apartment building, wishing Dad would change his mind. I felt some consolation knowing it was only going to be for a weekend. Thinking of Mom, I searched for a way we could leave Mom a clue as to where we were. I thought about the story of Hansel and Gretel and how they left a trail of bread crumbs so they could return home. I fantasized and day-dreamed for a few moments but could not think of a way to leave a trail, blissfully unaware that would be the last time I would see the apartment building. I turned around and faced forward to see the route to a journey ahead of me.

The drive to Maplewood from Minneapolis seemed longer than usual. Both Lorenzo and I were very quiet. Neither of us said a word enroute. When we got to Tia's house it was everything I had anticipated: pure chaos. Kids were running all over the place and everything was out of order. I began to cringe at thoughts of spending a night there, and dreaded spending a whole weekend with them. Dad dropped us off and left quickly.

The entire weekend I was nervous and did not think I was going to survive. I was so afraid of Shaft. When the dog looked at me, it seemed we nearly stood eye to eye. This dog and I had a mutual understanding. I did not like looking into his eyes and he did not like looking into mine. I avoided contact with Shaft as much as possible. Needless to say, Tia's kids thought it was amusing that I was afraid of the dog. Quickly, I became their entertainment. They decided to play a cruel trick on me.

Saturday afternoon, I had laid down on a bunk bed in one of the bedrooms to take a nap. Inwardly, I had convinced myself that taking a nap would make time go by faster. I was awakened by the sound of Shaft's wet wagging tongue and heavy breathing. There he was with his big eyes, stinky breath, and ferocious teeth in the room with me. He was lying on the floor next to the door with the door closed. I was trapped and felt so afraid I wanted to wet my pants. I did not know what to do. I gasped for air, took one big breath and as fast as I could climbed from the lower bunk bed to the top bunk. Shaft, who was startled by my sudden movement, jumped to his feet and started toward the bed while jumping up and down barking. I started crying and screaming as loud as I could.

Like a savior and protector, Lorenzo burst into the room and yelled, "Don't be afraid. I will get him out of here." He took Shaft outside and I just continued to sit there and cry. Once Shaft was tied up outside, my brother came back in the bedroom to console me. This was just one trick they played on me and Lorenzo.

Finally, Sunday came and I was so excited because I knew Dad was coming to pick us up. Night fell and I became even more excited because I thought Dad must be on his way. I felt some relief since I had made it through the weekend. I sat in the living room with my pink princess bag packed. Both my things and I were ready to go.

I waited for Dad while looking out the window and watching television. It got later and later. My eyes began to feel heavy. Dad still had not shown up. I had fallen asleep, when I heard the telephone rang. It was Dad. He called to tell us he could not come and pick us up and we needed to stay a few more days. I was heartsick. I thought I just needed to make it through the weekend. I told Dad I was afraid of Shaft and he told me he would not let the dog hurt me. I dared not tell my Dad what the kids had done to me for fear Dad's monster would appear. Also, I was fearful Tia's' kids might retaliate against me. They had already threatened me a number of times, saying if I told on them they would beat me up. Four of Tia's kids were teenagers and mean as rats. There was no persuading Dad. He would not come pick us up as he had promised.

The weekend turned into weeks, with Dad coming to visit us occasionally on the weekends. Dad brought more and more of our things with him, until all of our clothes and toys were with us. Mom had left us, and now Dad was leaving us, too. I felt so lonely, abandoned, neglected, and afraid. I retreated within myself as the kids continued to play mean tricks on us. I felt like Cinderella with her wicked step-sisters. There were times when Tia's daughters would feed us spoiled food while they ate good food. When they combed my hair it seemed like they were extra rough and would pull out my hair.

As each day went by I still looked for Mom's bright yellow Mustang to show up. Purposefully, I would stay outside for long periods of time, hoping she would drive down the street and see me. In my heart I kept wondering why she had not arrived yet. I missed her tremendously, but somehow could still sense her presence. Although Mom was gone, I believe there was a grace from God which made me feel like there was a portion of her with me still. Even if it was just in my memories, Mom was with me.

The memories of things we had done together remained in my heart – like making cakes with my Easy Bake oven or going special places, or being able to wear, play, and sleep in my black patent leather go-go boots when I was four and five years old. I thought about our red clogs we had just alike. She often made us matching outfits. Mom would sew for hours to make us special outfits to wear at family functions and special occasions.

Then, one day it happened. I received an impression in my heart from Mom. It was a special feeling. With my heart, I felt Mom's presence. I was following my routine of staying outside, playing and keeping a lookout for Mom's car to come down the road. Softly and gently, I heard Mom say, "I can't find you." This message gave me peace because my conscious and subconscious minds were in full combat. Like rats running to feed on garbage, thoughts ran through my brain. At times it seemed as if rats were finding their way into my secret place, the black box.

My conscious mind warred with my subconscious mind. They were warring over the fact whether Mom wanted me anymore. I began to doubt her love for me in my subconscious mind, but I knew Mom loved me in my conscious mind. In a secret compartment of the black box these thoughts were hidden: "If I was a good girl, maybe she would have taken me with her. Am I a good girl? If I am a good girl maybe she will come back for me. Santa Claus comes to good kids. Maybe Mom will come, too. Am I worth coming back for? AM I WORTHLESS? Mom packed her clothes and took them; why didn't she pack my clothes and take me?" The black box closed.

The thought of Mom's return continued to wake me up each morning and drive me to start my day. It was the only hope I had. The only thing

I could hold on to was...,"She's coming back for me." I held on tight to this hope. It was not long before it was time to start back to school. Dad came to visit us and explained we would attend school while living with Tia. As he was talking, I felt my body go numb and my voice became small. I wanted to tell him how horrible it was staying there and how we were being mistreated, neglected, and abused, but I was too afraid.

On one hand, I was afraid of how he would respond; on the other hand, I was afraid he would not respond at all. I had heard him say over and over, "I cannot take care of these kids," so I did not want to make it harder for him or deal with any more disappointment. If I had pleaded my case and Dad did not respond, I think I would have been more devastated. It was easier for me to conceal the abuse than to ask for help. In addition, there was domestic violence taking place in Tia's home as well. My father was aware of the physical fights which took place between Tia and my Uncle Charles; however, he seemed to be desensitized to the impact or potential danger we were in as children.

I felt like an orphan and instead turned my focus to Mom. Weeks and weeks had gone by and we had not talked to Mom since the day she left. Dad said he still did not know where Mom was, so we could not talk to her. We had to wait for her to call him. Dad was a messenger for us. He told us what Mom said and how she was doing. However, he would not tell Mom where we were so she could call and speak with us directly.

Once school started back I was in the first grade. I remember I had a difficult time concentrating and could not keep my mind focused on what the teacher was saying, doing, or teaching. Constantly, my mind was preoccupied all the time with fear about Mom's whereabouts and anticipation of her return. It was difficult to stay focused on what was going on in the classroom. The teacher would stand at the chalkboard and talk, but for me it was like the teacher talking on Charlie Brown, saying, "Wah wah woh wah wah."

I went from an above average student to average at best. I have very few memories of playing outside on the playground or with any of the kids in the classroom. I do not recall my teacher's name or any of the other students. Mentally, I was always preoccupied with anticipation of Mom's return. As the school year went on, I became more withdrawn from the other kids in class.

The most exciting part of the day and what I can vividly remember, was our red telephone in the classroom. It was new, shiny, and bright. Each time the telephone rang, suddenly I would stop what I was doing and focus on the teacher. She seemed as if she moved in slow motion toward the telephone. Sitting at attention, I listened carefully to the teacher as she answered the telephone, waiting for her to say who needed to report to the office. I believed and hoped every day that Mom would pick us up from school. I sat on pins and needles wishing for the teacher to call my name. She never did. Not only was I very attentive to the telephone, but I also watched our classroom door with great anticipation, hoping Mom was going to walk into the classroom and take me out of my misery.

In writing this book, I learned Lorenzo also focused on the same things. He was in another classroom and equally consumed by the telephone and door in his classroom. In looking and longing for Mom to return for us, we both suffered academically. Our unstable home life took a toll on both of us.

Nearly an entire year had gone by without Lorenzo or I being able to speak with our mother. Dad had intentionally cut off all direct lines of communication with Mom, which was one of the tactics he used in an attempt to force Mom to come back. It was so painful for me to be out of contact with her. I felt completely abandoned and like a stray dog no one wanted. Regularly, we asked Dad where Mom was and if she was coming back. His response was always the same. He said he was working on getting her back and he would come for us as soon as she returned.

Then, one day Dad took us out to see a movie. On the way back to Tia's house, my brother and I could no longer fight back the tears. We both broke down and began crying. We had been at Tia's house for about eight months and could not suppress or hide our feelings any longer. We sat in the car sobbing uncontrollably. Through tears and sobbing, as best we could, we told Dad we missed Mom and wanted to see her. Dad held onto us tightly and we cried together. He walked us into Tia's house promising he would find her for us and take us to see her for Mother's Day. Finally, we received relief and hope of being reunited with Mom. Weeks went by and nothing else mattered. We were going to see our Mom.

Dad held true to his promise. Within a few weeks he came with the good news. He had located Mom and we drove from Minnesota to Missouri to see her. I sat up front with Dad to help him stay awake. We talked about Mom and how we were going to be reunited as a family. All the way to Cape Girardeau, Missouri Dad explained how Mom would return with us. Our hopes and expectations were high. It seemed like a done deal; we were going to be a family again.

When we arrived in Cape Girardeau it was past midnight. We checked into a nearby hotel room and Dad and Lorenzo went to sleep. Dad was exhausted from our long drive. I was too excited to go to sleep so I lay still in bed, listened to Dad's snoring and waited for daybreak. Finally, day broke and sunshine filled our room. The sky seemed bluer than it ever had been before. I could hear birds singing and a fresh smell of spring was in the air. Dad woke up. It was past breakfast time so we ate the sandwiches we had packed.

After we got dressed, Dad called Mom for directions to her house, and we checked out of the hotel and drove over to Mom's house. It was a big beautiful home with a fenced-in backyard. We all went to the door and there she was. With a big smile and loving arms, Mom was waiting for us. Mom's boyfriend stood in the background watching as we were reunited. Lorenzo and I sat down on the couch with Mom. Lorenzo sat on her left side and I sat on her right side. Dad and Mom's boyfriend Duke stepped out of the living room and back onto the front porch.

My Mom had met Duke when we were living in Chicago. He'd lived in the apartment below us. He was a very handsome man with jet black hair, golden-brown skin and he spoke with a soft, smooth voice. He was hip and cool. I use to laugh at the gangster-style hats he wore. Duke would wait outside for us to get home. He seemed to always be around to offer his help with carrying groceries or opening doors or anything to get her attention. He'd often ask to walk us to the park. In the beginning, Mom would always politely decline his offers.

Duke finally caught a break when one day, our dog fell off our back porch and landed in his backyard. Pepper was just a stray dog we had found and started feeding. We kept her on the back porch. Mom had to knock on Duke's door and ask to retrieve the dog. After that, my mom seemed a little more cordial toward Duke, and began carrying on conversations with him. She started accepting some of his offers to help. He was always complimentary and would do some of the nicest things for her. Always the perfect gentleman, he was a breath of fresh air. I liked him a lot. He made me laugh. He called me "skinny mini" and joked with me all the time. I never heard him raise his voice too far above a whisper. But he was a man, a man I couldn't totally trust either. I felt I had to keep my eye on him, too.

Finally, both Lorenzo and I breathed a sigh of relief as we sat down and started talking with Mom. We told her how much we missed her, worried about her, and wanted to stay with her. It felt like the weight of the world had been lifted from my shoulders. We told her we were staying at Tia's house and hated it there. We asked why she did not come back for us. She said, "I searched and searched for you two but could not find you. I went to the community center and everywhere I could think of. I even went to the police department to see if they could help me, but they could not assist me in locating you two." I said, "Mom, Dad was hiding us from you, huh? He thinks you are going to come back with us."

In my heart I knew Mom was never going to return to us as a family. As we sat there and talked, tears begin to stream down my face. I was so happy to be reunited with Mom. As I looked into her eyes I could see she was in a safe place. The terror that had always gripped her was nowhere to be found. She had a degree of happiness and peace she had never had before. It seemed like even when we were having a good time in times past, there was always a darkness or cloud which overshadowed her. She would smile, but there was no depth to her smile. She was always smiling on the outside; however, looking deeply into her eyes, I could see pain and loneliness plagued her constantly. My brother and I grabbed onto Mom and held her as tightly as we could. We wept together.

It was Mother's Day. We had made gifts for Mom. Dad bought Mom's favorite chocolate candy. It was such a relief to know she was safe. There were no bruise marks on her face and she looked like herself again. We sat there and talked with her for what seemed like a few moments. Then with Dad's permission, Mom took Lorenzo and me on a walk to a nearby school which had a playground. We sat outside and talked, laughed, and hugged each other. It was the best day I had had since Mom's departure.

We walked back to Mom's house. Dad and Mom's boyfriend were still outside talking. My brother and I walked back into the house, and Dad asked Mom to stay outside for a moment. That's when he asked her. Dad asked Mom to come back to Minnesota with us. Mom stood there frozen. Contemplating her response, she looked at my Dad and then looked back at us. She was torn between two worlds. She was torn between life and death. She had to decide if she was going to exchange her life there for a possibility of a life with us, knowing she could and would be beaten and abused unmercifully. She was forced to make a decision no mother ever wants to make. She had to choose between her life and her kids. She paused and contemplated what to do. I could see she did not expect Dad to ask this question. She had been gone for nearly a year and was living with another man. I felt sorry for her.

Dad had put Mom in an awkward position by making Lorenzo and me two carrots. Here we were being dangled in front of Mom, a starving rabbit. Time stood still while Mom mustered up the courage and strength to respond. I wanted her to come back with us but I did not want her to come back all at the same time. I knew the monster would reappear.

While I hated it at Tia's house, there was and is no description for the torment I felt watching Dad physically abuse Mom. There was no pain greater than seeing Mom's face disfigured, eyes blackened, lips busted, and bruises on her body. Mom responded slowly and cautiously to Dad's question. She said, "No, I am not going back with you. I would like to keep the kids, but I cannot come back with you." I fell back on the couch and thought, "Here we go... the party is over. That was it."

To my surprise, Dad did not argue nor attempt to negotiate. Instead, he walked toward the door. He called for Lorenzo and me.

He said, "It is time for us to go."

Our visit was abruptly ended. We hugged Mom as tears welled up in our eyes. Dad went to the car and yelled for us to come on. My heart was heavy and it felt like a knife was in my throat. Mom turned to us with a look of devastation and disappointment. She kissed us on our foreheads and said, "Go on. You have to go now."

"When will we see you again," simultaneously we turned back to ask. After a short pause, Mom whispered, "I am going to work on it." We stepped out to the door and onto the front porch. By this time Dad was in the car with the engine roaring. Impatiently, he was waiting for us. Without emotions or expressions showing on our faces, we climbed into the car. I assumed my normal position in front. Lorenzo climbed in back. I wanted to cry but fought back my tears. Dad did not like tears. It was easier to stuff my feelings than risk having to deal with Dad's anger.

With Lorenzo and me in the car, Dad sped off like a bat out of hell. He always drove fast, but he was driving with a vengeance. Looking into his face, I could see hurt, anger, and disappointment were mixed together. I looked over at the speedometer needle and he was going over 100 miles per hour at times. He told me, "If I get pulled over by the police, you say you are sick and I am rushing you to the hospital."

Our drive back to Minnesota was a long one. I tried to sleep as much as possible. In my mind I had rationalized I would not have to talk with Dad or see the buried speedometer needle if I faked sleeping. I was afraid. Fear was a feeling I avoided getting in touch with. Using my imagination and pretense was a way to escape Dad, my fears, and unwanted emotions. As much as possible, I tried to remain still and pretended like I was sleeping. Lorenzo lay across the back seat and slept or played sleep, too. Lorenzo and I never talked about how we felt, but looking into his eyes I could see nothing but pain. He, too, longed to have stayed with Mom. He was afraid of the monster, too.

Dad drove all through the night. He pulled along the side of the road or into rest areas if he became too tired. He interrogated me some about what we had talked with Mom about. I gave him as much information as I could and it seemed to calm him down. Upon our arrival back in Minnesota we were taken back to Tia's house. It was just the way we had left it: chaotic. I did not mind the chaos as much because I had a new peace in my heart. Having seen Mom gave me a new courage and hope. It assured me she still had love for me. I learned she had tried to come back for us. It was comforting to know Mom still wanted us. What was most encouraging was to know Mom was safe. Mom's safety was more important than my own safety and comfort.

We continued to stay at Tia's house. Both Lorenzo and I did well enough in school to pass to the next grade level. Lorenzo completed the third grade and I completed first grade.

The next time we would see our Mom, the circumstances would be totally different and a pleasant surprise.

Chapter Seven
A Promise Fulfilled

Although we had not heard from our Mom since our visit on Mother's Day, I felt a sense of contentment. Mom had said she would work on us getting back together; therefore, I believed in my heart it would just be a matter of time before our nightmare would end. Not even the news of us having to stay at Tia's house for the summer could dampen my hope of reuniting with Mom. In my heart I was confident change was going to come, simply because Mom had said it would.

Summer at Tia's house presented some of the same old challenges: Shaft, mean teenagers, and my hair shedding. But, it also brought new ones. At school I at least knew I was going to have lunch. At Tia's house I never knew what to expect. Sometimes for lunch we would have a tablespoon of peanut butter. I did not like peanut better without jelly and bread but I quickly learned when you are hungry you will eat what's in front of you. Something was better than nothing.

As the summer began, I continued in my same pattern, spending as much time outside as possible. Each day I woke up hoping and believing this could be the day Mom would return for us. Constantly I was staying aware of my surroundings, hoping Mom's bright yellow Mustang would somehow magically appear. Underlying my hopefulness was a small ray of fear. Maybe she would not return for us.

While living with Tia, there was one place of refuge. There was a neighbor family which resembled what I longed for: a home with a loving family. I had one really nice friend in our neighborhood. When I was at her home the world seemed safe. She lived in a white house within 100 yards from where we were staying. Her hair was snow white blonde. Her parents were some of the nicest people you would ever want to meet. She had a sister who was a few years older than us and one older brother. When I went to visit her I felt like I was part of a family. We would play with her dolls and toys at her house. Visiting her home made me think of living as a complete family. I longed for what she had.

In my imagination I pretended like I did have that. I pretended for the moment we were sisters, and her family was my family, too.

The longer we stayed at Tia's house, it seemed like we became less and less of a priority for Dad. He hardly came to see us anymore. Phone calls replaced visits. Weeks would go by without seeing him. Nevertheless, Dad still did not allow us to talk with Mom or any of Mom's family members. My heart was completely broken by the separation from Mom. There were days where a sense of never-ending disillusion seemed as if it gripped the very essence of my being. Sometimes I would pretend in my mind it was just a bad dream, wishing one day I would wake up and be with Mom again. I felt completely abandoned and forsaken by both my parents.

My imagination became another place of refuge and comfort. Desperately I wanted to be with my mother. Every now and then I would imagine in my mind what the conversation was going to be like. Pretending and rehearsing the conversation in my mind or playing out scenes with dolls was a way of escape. All the while, in my heart, I felt Mom was looking for us. Still there were times it even felt like Mom's presence was with me. Once in a while it seemed like I could smell her scent. Today it is hard for me to describe it. The only thing I can rationalize is it was spiritual.

I was too afraid to tell Dad just how much I wanted to be back with Mom. I felt trapped. When I did try to talk to him about Mom, he would explain she was coming back and I just needed to be patient.

Lorenzo and I did not talk about how much we missed Mom to anyone, but one look could communicate the sadness, pain, and loneliness we both felt. We were in survival mode, living one day at a time and doing the best we could to make it through each day. We were very close to our Mom. Her absence bonded the two of us even closer together to her. Our relationship was the only stable aspect of our turbulent lives. Wherever Lorenzo went, I went. He made sure of it and so did I. We did whatever we could to parent, assist, and protect one another. We seldom parted too far from one another.

Here is just one example of how we attempted to parent and protect one another. Whenever there was a full plate of food at Tia's house, it came with a huge price; we had to eat everything on our plate. Sometimes that was a daunting task for me because the food did not always look appetizing. I could not stomach eating food that didn't look or smell good and I was not allowed to leave the table until everything on my plate was finished.

One time, after all the other kids had long since eaten and gone outside to play, including Lorenzo, I sat at the table for what seemed like hours staring at green, wilted, and slimy collard greens. In my six-year-old mind they were gross. Lorenzo played outside for awhile, then circled back around and came back to the table. With no one else around, he whispered,

"You can't eat it, can you?"

"Nope," I said.

"I'll help you."

In one swoop, he swiped the greens into a napkin, balled it up and walked quietly into the kitchen. He placed the napkin into the trash can and quickly ran out the door as if nothing had happened. This became a pattern for us. Anything I couldn't eat, he'd sneak back and either eat it or throw it away. My brother was my protector and brought a sense of comfort. I couldn't imagine going through life without him.

Today, it breaks my heart when I hear about kids growing up in traumatic situations and having to be split up from their siblings. I think that compounds the tragedy, because your siblings can become a safety net. They are possibly the only thing that is stable in an unstable environment. It scares me to think of what life would have been like without my brother. In hindsight, I do not think I would have fared as well. The bond we developed as a result of traumatic and turbulent circumstances has actually become a precious gift that has sustained us throughout our lives.

One day, all of us kids were hanging out in the basement watching television. I had to go to the bathroom so I told Britney, the oldest and meanest of Tia's kids. I proceeded up the stairs. As I turned the corner, headed towards the bathroom, I realized straight down the long hallway was the telephone. It was sitting out on a metal pedestal. It was a rare occasion to see the phone. The telephone was usually occupied by one of the teenagers or Tia had it kept hidden away in her bedroom. I was pleasantly surprised to see it out and no one was around.

Something on the inside of me leaped. I felt a sense of excitement. My mind raced. I thought to myself, "This is it! This is the moment I have been waiting for." Slowly and quietly, I proceeded down the hall past the bathroom. My heart began to pound as I anticipated talking with Grandma Maeomia. I felt excited and anxious all at the same time. Thinking I might get caught made me feel anxious. Imagining hearing Grandma Maeomia's voice excited me.

For a brief moment I contemplated what the older kids would do to me if they caught me. Tell Dad? Beat me? Pull my hair? Pinch me? They had done all those things enough times. In some ways I had developed a level of immunity to their abuse tactics, games, and torment. Taking a chance was worth the risk.

Before I knew it, I was there. I was standing right in front of the bright yellow telephone. Slowly and quietly I reached for the receiver. I held it in my hands, put the receiver to my ear, and listened to the dial tone. I had dialed Grandma Maeomia's telephone number so many times when we lived in Chicago that the number was still etched in my memory....434-4476. I dialed the number. I could hear the kids downstairs laughing. The television was turned up very loud. I looked around. I was still alone. I stood very still and waited. My heart pounded.

It seemed like I stood there for several minutes waiting for the telephone line to ring through. Nothing happened. Then suddenly an operator appeared on the line.

"Operator. What number are you dialing?"

I whispered to her, "I am trying to call my grandma. Her number is 434-4476. Then the operator began asking me questions.

"Are you home alone? Do your parents know you are dialing this number?"

I paused, held my breath and searched my mind for a response. I could not lie, but I could not tell the truth either. While I was still thinking, trying to come up with a response, she said, "That is not a working number." My heart dropped.

I became fearful and hung up the telephone abruptly. For a moment, I paused and contemplated what the operator was going to do. I was terrified; she would tell what I had done. I quickly went into the bathroom, closed and locked the door behind me. The bathroom was a place of safety. I listened to see if the telephone was going to ring. There was no sound outside of my heart pounding and heavy breathing. I gathered myself together and quietly rejoined the kids in the basement. Disappointment had engulfed me, but I pretended very well. I pretended like nothing had happened as I rejoined the kids in the basement. It had been close to a year since we had last spoken with Grandma Maeomia and I missed her so very much.

A few weeks later, Dad came by with a surprise. He had good news. We all were going to visit Grandma Maeomia in Chicago. I was so excited. Dad packed the car with a few of our clothing items, sandwiches, and fried chicken for the road. Off we went.

It was pitch dark when we left for Chicago. As we headed down the street in Maplewood, I was so glad to be leaving Tia's house even if it was just going to be for a weekend. I hoped we would never have to return.

The drive went by quickly. Dad was speeding the entire way. He told me I needed to stay awake to help him stay awake. He also needed me to be on the lookout for police cars. I was to pretend like I was sick if he got pulled over by the police. I stayed awake as best as I could, talking to him as much as I could. Both Dad and I loved music. We listened to oldies from the '60s and sang most of the way. Music was a place of refuge for Dad.

When we arrived in Chicago, it was the middle of the night. We headed straight to Grandma Maeomia's house. Words cannot express the excitement I felt as we drove through our old neighborhood. I missed our family. Memories of the kids we used to play with flashed through my mind. I had many fond memories of living in Chicago.

As we walked up to the front door I felt a sense of relief. I deeply sighed within myself. It was like I could rest and relax some. I could feel a sense of safety. As we got closer to the door, I thought to myself, "No one will hurt me here." Finally, we were going to a place where we would be accepted, loved, and cared for. Grandma Maeomia was going to protect and take care of us. She had a way of making everyone feel safe, special, and precious. I knew how much she loved my brother and me. We were her first grandchildren.

Whenever we were with her she would ask, "What do you two want me to cook you for dinner? What do you want for breakfast? Do you want to do this or that?" She always gave us choices and options. And, I never had to eat all the food off of my plate. If I did not like something, I did not have to eat it. I could hear love in her voice the way she called my name. She was the only one to call me "Nee-sa." In her Southern accent she would really draw out the "Nee" portion.

Dad knocked on the door. Grandma Maeomia was waiting for our arrival and had not been to sleep yet. She had such a warm and welcoming smile on her face as she immediately opened the door. She was wearing her blue nightgown and robe. Her hair was tied up in a scarf. I looked up into her big brown eyes. She still seemed larger than life. Her pretty light brown skin was glowing. She looked down at us with such love in her eyes. Then she stooped down and leaned in to us. She gave us the biggest hug and held us so tight. Her smell and authentic touch were refreshing and comforting. She kissed us on our cheeks as we embraced one another.

"I love you guys. I missed you guys," she said.

"We missed you, too," Lorenzo and I responded in unison.

I was surprised to hear Grandma Maeomia invite Dad inside. Because of the way he'd treated my Mom, she'd never liked him. And she never made this a secret. Nor did any of my Mom's other family members. In my father's presence, they were very kind and loving toward him.

Dad stood outside the door. He shook his head.

"I'm going to visit some of my friends. It's too late," Dad said.

"I am only in town for the weekend. I'll return for them Sunday," Dad said as he started to walk away.

Grandma Maeomia smiled, and kept saying to Dad, "I am so proud of you. You are such a good man, Hillie. I do not know what's wrong with that Lil." Dad basked in Grandma Maeomia's compliments for a few moments, thanked her, and left. I stood there and felt puzzled by her words. I recalled how often she spoke negatively of my father. In fact, I knew she could hardly stand to see him. It was grueling for her to carry on a conversation with him. I could tell deep on the inside she wanted to spit at the very sight of my father. I wanted to ask her why she was being so nice to him but I kept quiet.

We turned around and walked into the living room. It was in the middle of the night when we arrived so the house was quiet. Everyone was sleeping. It all looked the same. It was just the way it was when we had left. The furniture was the same. The smell of fried food lingered in the air. We sat at the kitchen table. Grandma sat in her usual seat, facing the oven. She had her coffee cup on one side of her, and her playing cards spread out for her favorite game, Solitary. On her left side was her crossword puzzle book. I would imagine this night she sat up playing solitary cards, drinking coffee, and working crossword puzzles while waiting for us to arrive. The kitchen is where our family conversations took place. We hardly ever sat in the living room. Grandma Maeomia had beautiful living room furniture, which was all covered in plastic so it would not get dirty.

We talked briefly with Grandma for awhile. She asked about where we were living. Then she gently reminded us that she had to leave for work in a few hours.

We put on our pajamas. Grandma Maeomia made a pallet on the living room floor. It was so peaceful in her home. Everything was neat, clean, and in order. No dishes were in the sink. The floors were freshly mopped. Each night before Grandma Maeomia lay down for bed, she mopped the kitchen floor.

I was tired from the drive and fell fast asleep as soon as my head hit the pillow. Suddenly, I was awakened. My aunts Doris and Bertha had come in. They were so surprised to see us there. It was like a reunion.

"What are you two doing here?" asked Aunt Doris.

Between yawns, I explained to them how Dad had let us come to visit.

"Oh, yeah. Does your mama know you're here?"

I shrugged my shoulders. "I don't know. My daddy said my mama don't want us. That's why she left us and that's why she won't come back."

In my heart I knew that wasn't really true, but it was what my father had told us sometimes when we asked him about her.

A puzzled look crossed her face. Auntie Bertha chimed in, "Huh... yo daddy is a liar. He's still holding y'all hostage. Oh, we gonna fix this!" Aunt Doris and Auntie Bertha talked back and forth as they grabbed our few belongings. Auntie Bertha stepped out of the living room into one of the bedrooms and called my Mom. It all felt confusing to me. Before I knew it, we were rushed out the door in our pajamas and into Uncle Walter's car. Grandma Maeomia was still fast asleep when we left.

Auntie Bertha did not live far from Grandma Maeomia's house. We headed over to her place. When we arrived at Auntie Bertha's apartment she quickly telephoned Mom. There, we were able to talk with Mom. I felt so excited. Mom was still in Missouri where we had seen her on Mother's Day. Her voice was upbeat. I could hear that she was excited to hear my voice. She immediately said, "I'm coming to get you."

"You promised you would come back for us," I said.

"I am coming tonight. When you wake up in the morning, I'll be there," she said. We were overjoyed with excitement. I said, "Really! Oh, Mom. You promise?"

"Yes, I promise," she said. Lorenzo and I started jumping on the bed and yelling at the top of our voices.

"Mom is coming! Mom is coming! Yeah!"

Auntie Bertha ran into the room to see what all the excitement was about. She did her best to get us to calm down.

"Okay, settle down. You have to go to sleep for her to come. So, you two need to get in the bed," she said.

"Okay, okay," we replied.

I looked at my brother and he had the biggest smile on his face. He glowed like the sun as we positioned ourselves in the bed and lay silently. Trying as hard as we could to go back to sleep, I closed my eyes. The world around me was full of joy. In my inner ear, I could hear Mom's voice saying, "When you wake up I'll be there." I imagined the smile on her face and her warm embrace as I heard these words again and again, "I'll be there." Mom always delivered on her promises.

The next day Mom fulfilled her promise. We were still sleeping when she arrived. I was awakened by the sound of her voice.

"Nissi… Nissi… I am here."

It felt like the weight of the world drained from my body. I felt free. I could finally breathe again. I felt safe and secure with the safety and security only a mother's presence could give. It took a few shakes to wake Lorenzo. When he opened his eyes and saw Mom's face, he broke into a contagious grin. It was a grin of relief and gratitude. It was a genuine smile, not like our phony clown smiles we had learned to wear so often before.

We both sat on the bed and talked with our Mom for what seemed like a few moments, but hours had gone by. It was a relief to finally be able to talk freely without any reservations or fear of repercussions for what we said. We knew with Mom we would not experience the dreadful interrogation process. We could express ourselves openly and honestly. We were free to be ourselves.

Before we realized it, noon had crept up on us. We were still in our pajamas. I was getting hungry. Lorenzo wanted to get more sleep so we let him take a nap. Mom got me some cereal and helped me get dressed. She washed and combed my hair. Growing up, I had a very sensitive hair scalp and would get sores sometimes. Mom checked my scalp and said, "No sores, but it seems like your hair has come out." I said, "Mom, they pulled it out. When they combed my hair they pulled on it hard until I would cry. Tia's girls did not like me. They said I talked too much."

Mom looked saddened by my comments.

"I am so sorry they hurt you. It won't ever happen again. I am going to take you guys back to Missouri with me."

Those words were music to my ears. My dream had finally become reality. It excited me to think we would never have to return to Tia's house. The nightmare was over.

"Really? Mom, we are going to live with you?" I asked.

"Yes," she responded.

We finished getting me dressed and went to visit some family and friends. Later we returned to Auntie Bertha's house where Mom took a nap. When Mom woke up from her nap, she said it was time for us to go. Mom and Duke (who would later become my stepfather) gathered our belongings.

We stopped by Grandma Maeomia's house before we headed to Missouri. Grandma Maeomia was at work but Aunt Jeannie and cousin Venessia were there. As we were getting ready to leave, I asked if Venessia could come with us. She was two months younger than me and, Venessia and I were very close. We had been brought up like twins. On days when Grandma Maeomia would take us to kindergarten, sometimes she would get our classrooms mixed up. She would send me to Venessia's class and Venessia to my class. We would try to tell Grandma Maeomia, but she would just tell us to hush.

Auntie Jeannie was Mom's younger sister by four years. She always looked up to Mom as her older sister and was happy to have her daughter join us. We quickly packed Venessia's belongings. The five of us – Duke, Mom, Lorenzo, Venessia and I – loaded into Mom's bright yellow Mustang and drove off. Grandma Maeomia had not made it home from work before we left. We did not get to tell her we were leaving.

We headed down the highway. All three of us kids sat in the back seat. I sat in the middle so I could see and hear everything that was going on. Duke was behind the wheel. I leaned forward and whispered to Mom, "Do you want me to stay awake and tell the police officer I am sick if we get pulled over?" She looked at me with a puzzled look on her face. She said, "No, that's okay. You do not have to stay awake." Hmmm... "Now that's different," I thought.

Riding with Duke was a different experience from being with Dad. Mom's speedometer needle was never buried, even though Duke was driving. I settled into the back seat with my brother and cousin Venessia. We were on the road for only a short time before it became pitch dark outside. It seemed like our car was the only light that illuminated the highway. I fell asleep leaning on my brother.

I felt so relieved to be with Mom again. Mom said we would go to school in Missouri and live with her permanently. It was comforting to know the nightmare of living at Tia's house was really over. It was all over. I thought about how things were going to be better.

When we arrived in Missouri it was late at night. We went straight to bed when we arrived. Mom had a room set up for us to sleep in. Her home was beautiful. Everything was clean and the furniture was new. The carpet was new, too. It smelled so fresh.

We slept later than usual the next morning. I was the first child to wake up. I could hear birds singing and smell the flowers that lined Mom's house. Mom was in the kitchen. She still had her pajamas on and was cooking breakfast. I was hungry. I walked into the kitchen and sat at the kitchen table. I liked watching Mom cook. She was cooking our favorite, French toast.

As I watched Mom, she seemed to move slower than normal. Her gestures were methodical. She seemed to be deep in thought. I could see something about her had changed. She was my Mom. But she was different. It seemed like a different kind of fear lightly painted her face. She looked older. She did not have the vibrancy she once had. I asked her, "What's wrong, Mom?" She turned around and smiled. Looking back at me, she said, "Oh, nothing. I am just glad you are here." Her nonverbal gestures spoke louder than her words. I knew something was wrong, but I was not sure what.

Duke entered the kitchen from the back door. He seemed distant and cold. Duke had changed, too. He did not greet me with a warm bubbly smile as he had done in the past. He was funny, playful, and joyous when we lived in Chicago. He did not call me "skinny mini, skinner than a penny." There were no jokes this morning. There was a silence and uneasiness in the atmosphere as he simply said, "Good morning."

As I sat at the kitchen table, I watched them interact. I perceived something was wrong. Before I knew it, my mind started racing. I felt afraid. I felt all alone. I felt like an outsider with Mom. I blurted it out, "You're trying to take my mama away from me. You're trying to take her away." The tears welled up in my eyes. Mom was standing in the kitchen but there was a gulf between us. We did not have the same connection we once had. It felt like the connection they had was stronger than my connection. I was an outsider. I felt abandoned. I felt like Mom loved him more than me. We were once her world.

I ran from the breakfast table with tears gushing from my eyes. Mom and Duke stood still in front of the stove without a response from my outburst. Quickly, I ran into the bathroom and slammed the door shut. I could be alone in there. It was safe in the bathroom. No one would come in. It was too painful for me to come out.

A few minutes later, there was a knock at the door. The knock was ever so soft. By the sound of the knock I knew it was Mom. I was hurt. I was angry. I did not want to talk or see her. I said, "I got to use the bathroom." I heard her footsteps walk away from the door.

I stayed in the bathroom as long as I could and cried quietly. I heard the other kids moving around. They needed to get in the bathroom. I pulled myself together and washed my face. I walked out of the bathroom, but on the inside I was still hiding. I hid by not sharing my hurt, pain, disappointment, fears, and frustration. The black box was opened. A message was placed on the inside. It said, "She's gone. Things will never be the same again." The thoughts floated over and over until they were deposited into the black box. The black box closed and disappeared.

We spent the rest of the morning unpacking, watching television, and getting used to our new surroundings. Later in the afternoon, we all went with my Mom to the Save-a-Lot grocery store. She bought all the snacks we liked and lots of fruits and vegetables. We played in her large, grassy backyard, while Mom watched us from the kitchen window. Duke grilled hamburgers and hot dogs on the grill for dinner. We watched television until we could not stay awake any longer. We were all in a period of adjustment. Everything was different and new. I loved our new home. It was the nicest home we had ever lived in. It wasn't like it was in Chicago. It could never be again, because we were different. We weren't like we were in Chicago. Duke knew. My mother knew. I knew. Lorenzo knew.

During the rest of our time together, my mother never said anything about my outburst. Neither did I.

CHAPTER EIGHT
SEARCH FOR MISSING CHILDREN

Cape Girardeau was a serene town, where you could hear the sound of crickets at night. It was rich with green countryside roads. The people were friendly and everything about it spoke of peace.

We had been at my Mom's house in Cape Girardeau for about a month and the time had flown by so quickly. After the initial awkwardness, we settled into a routine. A few days after we arrived, Duke's six-year-old son, Dewey, came to visit. Even though he was closer to my age, he and Lorenzo spent much of the time playing together, and Venessia and I were inseparable.

It was summer and all of our days were spent pretty much the same. We got up, had breakfast, and played. Later we would clean our room and get dressed. My mother would prepare lunch in the afternoon and we'd eat and play some more. We usually had dinner around six o'clock. After that, we'd watch television until bedtime. Mom took us everywhere she went. On Fridays we went to the Goodwill and each picked out a toy or a book for the week. We picked more toys than books. We were having the time of our lives, with no violence, no abuse, and no arguments.

It was Saturday night, August 2, 1975. The memories of this night are in Technicolor for me. Unexpectedly, I was abruptly awakened from sleep when I heard a thump… thump… sound outside of the window. I was lying next to the window and it was open. It was a hot summer night, so we left the windows open for ventilation. I lay their quietly and very still. Feeling afraid, I wondered in my mind what that sound could be. Then like a flash of lightning, it dawned on me as the thump, thump continued. Someone or something was outside the window. I dared not move. I thought maybe it was a robber. I just lay there and pretended like I was sleeping, hoping they would go away.

The four of us kids had been having a blast with my mother and Duke. It was me, Lorenzo, our cousin Venessia, and Dewey all lined up across the floor in front of the television. We had the whole living room to ourselves and decided to make tents. All our tents had fallen down and magically covered us. We had stayed up as late as we could to watch television. It was so much fun. Eventually, we all had fallen asleep. My mother must have turned the television off for us.

Lying there on the floor, I could not figure out who was outside the window. Too fearful to look out the window, I kept my eyes open just a little so I could see what was happening. Then I heard footsteps. There was quietness. I opened my eyes, feeling a little safer. Then suddenly he appeared. I saw a man standing on the front porch looking in on us through the glass front door window. I could not see his face clearly, because the sheer curtains hanging on the door somewhat masked his face.

My mind raced as he stepped closer and closer to the door. Then he pressed his face and hands up against the glass so he could get a better look. He was wearing black leather gloves on his hands. I could no longer deny reality. As the man peered through the glass, all my doubts were eliminated. I knew who it was. It was my father. I was terrified.

I lay very still on the floor, wishing I could hide in the darkness and stillness of the night. Dad's body filled the door frame. It felt like his eyes were in 3-D as he scanned the room. His eyes searched the whole room and I sensed it as he identified us on the floor. I wondered if he knew I was awake. I held my breath, feeling afraid he might hear me breathing. Dad's hands moved slowly toward the door knob and he turned it gently. Without it making a sound the door handle moved. I was very relieved the top deadbolt lock was on.

I watched as Dad slowly and quietly backed away from the front door and disappeared in the darkness of the night. I heard him pass by the window again and then it became quiet. The sounds were gone. I could faintly hear the crickets chirping in the background again. I dared not move as my mind continued to race… "Dad is here… Oh no, Dad is here." I breathed slowly, lying on the floor in the same position and being very quiet, not knowing if he would return. I was too afraid to move, let alone get up and tell Mom what I had seen. I stayed awake as long as I could, then drifted back to sleep.

The next morning I awakened to the smell of pancakes and sausage cooking on the stove. The birds were singing and the fresh aroma of gardenias filled the air. I got up and started toward the kitchen.

"Good morning. Did you sleep well?" asked my mom.

Mom was standing at the stove watching the sausage cook. "Good morning," I replied slowly. I sat there staring into space. I debated whether or not to tell her the bad news. I was afraid to tell her what I had seen the night before.

I sat at the kitchen table and watched her. Softly, I said, "You know what, Ma?" "What?" she asked. I felt a lump in my throat and wanted to cry. "Ma, Daddy is here." Looking down at me with her beautiful chocolate brown eyes and a puzzled look, she said "Huh." I repeated myself, "Ma, Daddy is here. I saw him last night. He was here. You know when I was lying on the floor I heard a noise outside the window. It was like thump, thump and I was scared. So I just lay on the floor and pretended like I was sleeping and then the next thing I knew, when I opened my eyes again there he was. Daddy was standing right there in the doorway. He was looking for us through the glass door. Mom, I just lay there and pretended like I was asleep."

"Oh, okay," Mom replied. She nodded her head and turned around. She went back to watching the sausage cook on the stove. It did not seem like it was a big deal to her. She did not get upset and I did not cry. Mom just went on with business as usual. She quickly changed the subject. She asked, "Do you want to go to church today? You know today is Sunday. The bus comes around 8:30 a.m. if you want to go." I replied, "Yes, I want to go."

I loved going to church. I liked meeting new children from across the city, attending Sunday school and the special glazed donuts we received for attending. Donuts were a special treat and incentive enough.

I sprang from the table to run to the bathroom. While I was in the bathroom I heard the telephone ring. The telephone was so loud it sounded like a siren. I wondered who was calling us so early on a Sunday morning. The telephone hardly ever rang. Usually when the telephone rang it meant something was wrong. I listened to Mom's voice saying, "Hello." From the sound of her voice I sensed it was not good news on the other line. I quickly finished up in the bathroom and washed my hands.

When I arrived back in the kitchen, I could hear Mom talking.

"Yea, they're here. No, my mother did not have anything to do with this. She didn't know what was going on. They're fine. Oh yeah, we're having a good time," she said. My Mom's face had grown pale as she talked. She seemed taken aback by the caller. I stood there as she talked. I felt sadness in my heart. I knew, by Mom's responses, it was Dad on the other line. By this time, we had been with Mom for about a month without any communication from Dad.

Mom motioned for me to draw closer to her.

"Yea, she's right here. No, he's still sleeping. I need to get the other kids up for breakfast. Mmmmm... huh, oh, okay. Here, you can talk to her," my mother said as she handed me the telephone.

I could feel the lump in my throat. I wanted to cry. I whispered, "Hi Daddy." I stuffed my emotions and cried on the inside. I feared the monster was back again. I pleaded within myself, "Please do not hurt anyone, Daddy. Please do not hurt us."

"How's my princess?" he asked.

Although he sounded happy and cheerful, I knew my Dad was not happy about us being there. For a moment I was speechless. It took a few moments for me to get my thoughts together so I could respond to him.

"Good," I responded. I knew an interrogation would probably follow. Frantically, Dad started in with questions.

"Are you having fun? What have you been doing? Where's Duke? What is he doing?" He went on and on, pausing only to catch his breath. I interrupted him and quickly said, "I saw you in the doorway last night. Are you here?"

There was silence on the other end. "Yes, I am here. But you cannot tell anyone, Nissi. This has to be our secret. I saw you guys sleeping on the living room floor last night."

It was those words which shut down my voice. With a soft whisper I said, "Dad, I heard you outside the window, too."

"I am here to get you guys," Dad responded.

There was a heartfelt darkness that entered the room as I fretted over Dad's statement, "I am here to get you guys." The thought of returning to Tia's house caused me to sink into a quicksand of dread. I was fearful that Dad's appearance meant a fight.

By Dad's telephone call, his appearance on the porch, and the determination in his voice, I knew he meant business. This also meant Dad would not allow any obstacles to get in his way or stand between him and us. What Dad said, what Dad did, was law. It was going to happen. There was no doubt in my mind.

Just the thought of Dad coming to the house with the intention of taking us was frightening to me. We had had a whole year without witnessing the appearance of the monster or Dad's demons. While living with Tia, being apart from Mom, and having no communication with her made 1974-75 the most difficult year of my life, it felt better than witnessing Mom being abused.

As a small child, my greatest comfort was found in one thing: Mom's safety. This was more important to me than my own sense of well-being and security. As long as I knew she was safe, I felt some sense of security. Even though I was only seven years old, I was very aware of what was going on. I worried about Mom continually. I was troubled over her safety. At times, I was so frightened and worried about Mom's safety that it was often hard to focus or concentrate on anything normal. My greatest fear was that someone would be killed. I feared either my mother or father was going to die because of the monster.

Instantly, as I stood there in silence, the black box opened. Scenes I had hidden away in the black box so carefully began to flutter through my mind, like clips from a movie scene. My conscious mind was plagued with memories of Mom and Dad fighting. I felt anxiety surfacing, and my hands began to sweat. My face became hot.

I wanted to shout, "This is where we are supposed to be. This is what was supposed to happen. We expected to be with Mom. I told you, Mom said she would come back to get us and now she has come." I was too afraid to voice my feelings, for fear of provoking the demon. The black box provided for another response.

Suddenly there was a news flash in my mind.

"Duke has a gun. He knows how to shoot it, too. He goes hunting. He kills rabbits and everything," out of nowhere I whispered.

"Really?" Dad said.

It was a desperate effort to protect us all. I was hopeful I could spark fear in my Dad and hold him at bay. His response gave me the courage to proceed.

"Yep! Daddy, the gun sits right next to the refrigerator. You can see it."

I was telling the truth, too. It was a long, double-barrel shotgun. I sneaked and touched the barrel once and it felt very cold. But I did not pick it up because I was told not to touch it. As a small child, I was very familiar with the power of a gun.

In May of 1968, just two months after my birth, Dad suffered a gunshot wound to his head and shoulder. He nearly bled to death due to the injuries he suffered. He was shot while leaving work one night. As he was walking out of the grocery store where he worked, someone shot him. Apparently, the shooter was on top of an adjacent building. The shooter shot randomly into the crowd of employees leaving the grocery store.

Unfortunately, the exact details surrounding the circumstances and shooter are unknown to us still to this day. Keep in mind the year was 1968. That year was marked with unrest in the African-American community. Both Reverend Martin Luther King Jr. and Robert Kennedy were assassinated just months apart. One was shot in April, and the other in June, respectively.

Dad's case was given nearly no attention, since it was a considered a "black on black" crime. He lived in the inner city of Chicago, so police investigators may have seen it as a waste of time to proceed with an investigation. Due to the gunshot wound, Dad was rushed to the hospital. He had to undergo numerous surgeries to reconstruct his face and lower jaw. The nine millimeter bullet hit him in the face and went right through his lower jaw, knocking out many of his teeth, and shattering his jaw bones in multiple places. The bullet exited his face on the right side and lodged into his right shoulder. I was too young to be aware of his countless surgeries; however, the scars remained on his face and were very visible. This too contributed to my fear of him. People would often stare at him because of his scarring, disfigurement, and missing teeth.

My conscious mind re-engaged and the black box closed. Inwardly, I was still agonizing over what was going to happen next, when we were interrupted by Lorenzo joining us on the telephone line. As my brother picked up the other line, Dad asked him several questions and made small talk. I was ready to end the conversation. I wanted to run and hide so he would not find me, but I felt there was no place I could hide.

Remembering that I wanted to go to church, I interrupted them and asked Lorenzo if he wanted to go, too. Lorenzo said, "If you go, I'll go with you."

Looking fearful, puzzled, and confused, Mom hurried back into the kitchen. She rushed us off the telephone saying it was time for breakfast. We said our usual "so long" to Dad. As a family, we had a tradition Dad had taught us. The tradition was never to say good-bye to one another. We used instead the statement, "so long," meaning it will only be "so long" until we meet or see each other again. Dad felt saying good-bye was too permanent of a statement. We said, "so long" and hung up the telephone.

I sat at the kitchen table feeling deflated. Mom said I had to hurry for the bus would come to pick us up shortly. I ate my breakfast quickly and started getting ready for church. I got dressed as fast as I could. We kissed Mom on the cheek as both my brother and I headed out the door. I said nothing to anyone about Dad's secret. I knew he would come for us, but I was too afraid to tell anyone.

The large yellow bus stopped near our block, just across the street from Mom's house. I enjoyed riding the school bus. It made me feel like I was older. In Chicago we had lived so close to school that we walked there.

When the school bus arrived, Lorenzo and I climbed aboard as Mom watched us from the front porch. We found a seat on the bus and sat together. We had gone to this church for a few Sundays, so we were familiar with the routine. As the bus drove away, I looked back and

Mom was still standing on the porch. She waved at us. I wondered if I would ever see her or her house again.

It was Sunday, August 3, 1975. The day was beautiful. It was sunny, bright, and hot. We arrived safely at church and went to our Sunday school classes. It was hard for me to focus on the teacher. I kept thinking about seeing Dad. I thought about what he had said. I looked for him to come for us. I felt confused and so disappointed because I did not want to leave Mom. I hoped no one would get hurt.

I do not remember what the teacher taught on that particular day. They usually taught about Jesus. One thing I do recall very vividly is the teacher asking if anyone wanted to ask Jesus into their hearts. I raised my hand. I felt my own fears, desperation, and loneliness. I hoped Jesus could help us. I remembered how Mom would stay at the altar praying for long periods of time.

There was no doubt in my heart I wanted to be with Mom, but matters were different than before. My mother had Duke in her life now. I knew circumstances were beyond me. When Sunday school was dismissed, we were ushered into the main sanctuary for the regular church service. After the choir sang, the pastor preached a long sermon. I had a hard time focusing on the message. Because we'd stayed up so late the night before, my eyelids grew heavy. I tried hard to keep them open, but I just couldn't. I was nodding when the pastor asked for those who wanted to receive Jesus to come forward. My teacher nudged me and escorted me up front. I wasn't alone. There were a lot of people giving their hearts to Jesus that day. There were other kids from other classes, too. Lorenzo cracked a smile as I passed him on the way to the altar.

The pastor asked us to bow our heads as he prayed. I prayed that Jesus would save my mother and us from my father. When the pastor finished praying, we were ushered back to our seats and soon afterward, the service was dismissed.

Along with all of the other children from the neighborhood, Lorenzo and I climbed back on the school bus. We headed for home. Right before exiting the bus, we were given the opportunity to select a freshly-baked glazed donut. We each took one.

Finally, we were back in my mother's neighborhood. As I got off the bus, I looked at Mom's house. Everything seemed calm and peaceful.

Being very aware of my surroundings, I checked to see if my Dad's car was in the driveway. I saw nothing — no car, no Dad. I felt we were safe. We raced across the street. I followed Lorenzo through the front door. I glanced back to see the yellow school bus one last time. As I looked, there behind the school bus was a four-door black 1968 Chrysler Newport. It was Dad in his car waiting behind the bus. His car was shiny and spotless as usual. It looked like the Batmobile. My heart pounded. I gasped, slammed the front door, and locked it.

Mom was sweeping the kitchen floor when we walked in. Venessia and Dewey were in the backyard playing. Lorenzo quickly ate his donut and rushed out the back door to join them.

I sat at the table, slowly ate my donut, and stared at my Mom. There were no bruises on her face or arms. She seemed happy. I wondered if I should tell her about Dad. I didn't know how she would respond. I didn't want to upset her. With all my heart, I wished my father would just leave us alone.

"Can I help you?" I asked my mother.

"Sure, run and get the dust pan for me. It's in the back closet."

Emotionally, I felt confused. I could sense Dad pulling at my heart. He wanted us all. He wanted to have his family back. He wanted everything to be as it was. I longed to stay with Mom but felt like we were a problem for her.

I went and got the dust pan and held it down while Mom swept trash into it. That's when I could see the pain in her face. She was crying on the inside. Perhaps she was still disturbed by Dad's telephone call. Maybe she was hoping Dad was going to let us stay with her without a fight. Or maybe she and Duke were having problems because of us.

Naturally, I internalized my mother's disturbance. I felt like we were the problem. Maybe she would be better off without us being there. Maybe Dad would leave them alone. Like a pawn on the chess table, I felt we were possibly the trade.

The next move was up to me. Inwardly, I struggled. The black box opened. My conscious mind determined it was best to say nothing. My subconscious mind haggled; were we causing my Mother problems with Duke? The black box tried the case and made a judgment.

My conscious mind asked, "What is the verdict?" The black box responded, "You are the problem. Duke does not really want you guys here. Mother is safe now."

Still holding the broom in her hand, I watched my Mom as she continued to sweep trash into the dust pan.

My serious internal debate was interrupted by Lorenzo, Venessia, and Dewey's abrupt entry into the house from the backyard. The black box disappeared.

"We want to have a party! Can we Mom?" shouted Lorenzo. My mom stood up, thought about it a second, then nodded her head that we could.

"We need to go to the store to get party stuff," cried Venessia.

My Mom disappeared into the bedroom, removed two crisp one-dollar bills out of her purse and returned. She handed the money to Lorenzo and said we each could spend fifty cents.

There was nothing that could divert my focus from my terrible woes faster than candy. Lorenzo, Venessia, Dewey, and I sprinted to the front door.

"Make sure you look both ways when you cross over Williams Street," my mother called out from the porch. We were already halfway down the block, running and skipping.

The small convenience store sat on a corner a block away from my mother's house. Bells hanging on the door jingled softly, announcing our entrance into the store. The interior was small and jammed-packed with shelves of food and all sorts of items. We each picked several items. I grabbed a bag of Lay's potato chips and my favorite watermelon "Now and Later" candy. The others got two cans of Pepsi, popcorn, and an assortment of other candies. Our plan was to share everything we bought. Lorenzo handed the cashier the two crisp dollar bills. We had a few pennies left over, so the cashier said we could buy some penny candy with the change. We bought a few more pieces of licorice candies and bolted from the store.

We stopped at the corner of Williams and Hanover Street. I stuffed my Now and Later candies into my pocket. Williams was a busy, four-lane street. After looking both ways, Lorenzo directed us across. Back on my mother's block, Hanover Street, we headed toward home, giggling and laughing the whole way. Dewey walked a little bit ahead of us. Venessia and I walked side by side. Lorenzo trailed behind us, keeping watch. He was the oldest.

We were only two or three houses away from my mother's house when a car sped down the street and came to a screeching halt near us. Terrified, we stopped dead in our tracks. I looked out of the corner of my eye; the car was a black Chrysler Newport, my father's car. I quickly looked inside the car and there was my Uncle Charles hovering over the steering wheel. His fingers were grasping tightly the steering wheel. There was a look of confusion and panic on his face. Dad was in the passenger seat. He opened the door and jumped out yelling at us, "Get in the car! Get in the car!"

In my heart I wanted to faint as fear gripped me. I was so afraid. The black box was opened. I could hear my conscious mind saying, "Run, run, run. Run as fast as you can." I felt confused. The following messages were placed in the black box, "There are no safe places to hide. You can never hide from him. He will always find you. No fear; now is not the time to be afraid. Do not let your true emotions show."

Before I knew it my legs began to move and I started running across the street as fast as I could. Frantically, I searched down the block. I was hoping Mom would walk out the front door of her home but there was no motion or sound coming from that direction. Stillness lingered in the atmosphere. We were all alone to face Dad's demon. As I looked to my left, there was an elderly man and woman sitting on their porch in their rocking chairs. They watched us with their mouths wide open. I did not run to them because I was afraid Dad might hurt them.

I ran away from Dad and I ran away from his car. I ran away from everyone. In the corner of my eye I could see Lorenzo standing, frozen in place on the sidewalk as I stepped off the curb and onto the street paved with black tar. Lorenzo's eyes were the size of a saucer. I had not told Lorenzo about what I had seen and heard the night before, so he was even more caught off guard by Dad's presence. He was frightened at the very sight of Dad. Lorenzo was horrified by the sound of Dad's commanding voice. While I worked diligently to mask all my fears, Lorenzo was not as deceiving.

Swiftly, Dad grabbed Lorenzo in one swoop with his right arm. He carried Lorenzo like he was a twenty pound sack of potatoes and threw him into the car. Frantically, I was still taking flight and trying to find a place of safety when I felt Dad's strong forearm wrapped around my waist. Suddenly, I knew it was all over. He had caught me. Dad picked me up with one arm and pulled me tightly to his chest. His heart was pounding. We were both breathing hard. I was pinned between his forearm and chest as he held on to me tightly. In a few quick steps, we were back at his car.

I felt like no one could really help us.

Venessia stood in a comatose state frozen on the sidewalk. She had watched everything take place. She knew my Dad and was afraid of him, too. Dewey looked like a lost puppy, unsure of what to do next.

Dad put me in the backseat and quickly slammed the car door. As he got in the front seat, he gazed at Venessia. She was petrified. With a smile on Dad's face he asked her if she wanted a ride back to Chicago. Venessia was too scared to respond. I loved Venessia so much. I was afraid for her. She was a shy and a quiet girl. Venessia did not talk as much as me. With her eyes filled with tears she looked at me. I shook my head "No." She got the message and shook her head to my father. Seeing her shake her head very slowly, I leaned back into the leather seat of the car and breathed a sigh of relief. She was safe.

Uncle Charles sped off. I turned around on my knees in the backseat to see Mom's pale mustard-colored house one last time. I watched Dewey and Venessia run down the block. Dewey swung the front door wide open.

Immediately, Uncle Charles began yelling at Dad.

"Man, you shouldn't have done that! I thought you were going to go up to the door and ask for the kids. Man, this is kidnapping! The police are going to come after us. They're gonna find us! We're going to jail for this! We can't get away!"

I leaned forward in my seat. Dad was breathing heavy. He was in a state of panic. The car quickly filled with anxiety. I could hardly breathe. I felt afraid. Suddenly I blurted out, "He has a gun. Duke has a gun."

The car became silent. The anxiety which had filled the vehicle began to dissipate. Dad whispered in a childlike voice, "I had to do it like that."

There was nothing more said. I slid back into my seat and took a deep breath. I felt so torn up inside. The black box opened. I wanted to cry but instead hid my feelings deep inside the black box. I longed to be with both of my parents without violence.

Before I knew it, we went down several side streets and were back on the highway headed back to Minnesota.

We drove in silence. Then my Dad turned around and looked at Lorenzo, then at me. I knew what was coming, the interrogations. I dreaded Dad's questioning because the wrong answer could cause the demon to appear. Being the spokesperson, Dad naturally began with me.

"Why didn't you run and get into the car, Nissi?"

"Huh."

I started acting like I did not hear or understand Dad's question. This was a way for me to buy more time to respond. I definitely needed more time to think of how to respond to this question. The truth would infuriate Dad.

"Why did you run away from me?"

I could not tell the truth and I could not tell him a lie either. Inside I knew I ran away from him because I did not want to leave with him. With a puzzled look on my face, I paused long and thought hard. I felt the knife held to my throat. I contemplated how I would respond to the monster. I slowly started shrugging my shoulders, as if I did not know why I had run from Dad. I summoned the black box and was searching for a response when Dad answered his own question.

"Did you get confused? Did you not recognize my car? Did you not recognize me?"

At seven years old I felt I needed to pretend with my father. I had learned to pretend like I was happy and agree with him quickly. He needed lots of encouragement and support. There was no time for tears. Tears and disappointment expressed to Dad fueled his anger. By this time I was a professional at hiding my true feelings deep inside the black box. I felt I had to remain emotionless. With caution, I looked into his eyes and did the forbidden. I lied.

"Yes, I was confused. I did not realize it was you and your car."

Whew... I was so grateful Dad gave me an out. Like loading a gun, Dad had loaded my lips with an acceptable response.

I slid back into my seat as the interrogation continued. Dad had many questions about what we did, Mom's boyfriend, etc. I entertained all his questions and fired off responses as quickly as Dad asked them. As Lorenzo sat on the other side of the back seat, he leaned up against the door. His eyes were closed and he pretended like he was asleep. I was afraid for Lorenzo and wondered if he wanted to jump out of the car. We were moving too fast to escape. I felt cold and lonely on the inside. We left with only the clothes on our backs. Dad eventually ran out of questions and turned to face the road.

In my heart, I wanted to cry but there was no place I could do so without Dad seeing me. So like always, I suppressed my feelings. I reached into my pocket and pulled out my Now and Later candies. I found comfort in my candies; they were familiar and sweet. I unwrapped them slowly and ate them one at a time. I neatly folded the wrappers and placed them in the ashtray in the side door of the car.

As we drove, it became pitch dark and began to rain. Thunder clapped its hands. Lightning flashed its power. At times, rain invaded the road in a downpour and made visibility poor. We had to pull over on the side of the road several times. Grandma Maeomia always told us to be still when there was thunder and lightning because God was talking. Grandma Maeomia never lied so I believed her. This night I imagined God was not only talking, but God was crying. God was crying for me all the tears I wanted to express but couldn't, crashing onto our car and the pavement. God cried for me.

On the way back to Minnesota, I worried and dreaded returning to Tia's house. I drifted off to sleep to the sound of rain. I was pleasantly surprised when we arrived in Minneapolis. We did not return to Tia's home. Instead we went to live with Dad's sister, Jane, who had moved to Minneapolis. She had a two-bedroom apartment located just a block away from Hans Christian Anderson Elementary School, which we would attend in the fall.

Until writing this book we never told Dad we were being abused at Tia's house. We never spoke about all the things that happened at Tia's. The memories were hidden in my black box. Thankfully, we never again returned to Tia's house to live.

PART TWO

THE "BLACK BOX" WAS IN COMMAND—HOW WITNESSING FAMILY VIOLENCE IMPACTED ME

CHAPTER NINE
CHILDHOOD LETTERS TO
MY MOM....

Life with Aunt Jane was considerably more functional and a lot less chaotic than Tia's house. We were not mistreated or abused by her. Mama Jane reminded us of a comic book superhero. She was slim and trim. She had light, golden-brown skin and big, dark brown slanted eyes. We loved Jane dearly. She loved us, too. There was no violence taking place at her home. Our life with her was relatively peaceful. We all worked together diligently to keep the apartment tidy and clean.

A new school year started a few weeks after arriving back in Minneapolis. It was our fourth school in three years. Jane compelled Dad to go out and buy us new shoes, clothes, and school supplies before the beginning of the school year. Second grade was a difficult year but a much better year for me in comparison to my first grade school year. In the beginning of the school year I was rather withdrawn and subdued most of the time. I spent the majority of my time watching and observing those around me. I hardly talked in school. When we had recess outside, I still watched every car that passed, looking for my Mom.

My intense search for Mom lessened as the year progressed. In my heart I knew she would never find us now. It took awhile, but I made two good friends. Teresa and Lisa sat near me. Teresa had thick dark red hair, rosy cheeks, and big freckles. Lisa had light-brown skin and a perfectly round face like a circle. Her hair was black.

While things were less than perfect living with Jane, it was a thousand times better than living at Tia's house. With Jane we always had good food to eat and there were no strict rules like having to eat everything on your plate. However, at Jane's house I learned about marijuana. Jane, Dad, and Jane's girlfriend sometimes got high together. I did not like the smell of marijuana but grew accustomed to it. At Jane's, I also learned about homosexuality. Jane was living a lesbian lifestyle at the time. Jane had a few "straight" friends but most of her friends were homosexuals. Up until that time, I had never been exposed to the homosexual lifestyle, so it seemed strange and foreign to me.

Jane had children. One of her sons took a special liking to me. He was a few years older than Lorenzo and four years older than me. His name was Jon. Jon treated us like we were his little brother and sister. Jon was short, stocky, full of funny jokes, and energy. Unfortunately, it was through Jon that I first learned about molestation and sexual abuse, though I didn't comprehend it at the time. At night sometimes, Jon would crawl in bed with me and stick his hand up my gown and fondle me, etc. He assured me everything was okay, and warned me to keep my mouth quiet. He said I would only get in trouble if I told anyone. Until now, I have never told. It was all pretty confusing to me and more than I could comprehend. Besides, I felt there was no one I could tell. I still didn't feel safe or secure.

Just like when we lived at Tia's house, we were again in hiding from my Mom. All lines of communication were cut off from Mom. We were like pawns in my Dad's hands. Mom could talk with Dad and had a way of reaching him; however, she had no way of reaching us. Daddy still did not live with us. Nor did he take us to where he lived. We had no idea where he lived. Dad would come and visit us much more than he did when we lived in Maplewood. When we would get up enough courage, we would inquire about our Mom. Sometimes Dad would say he had spoken to her, but most of the time he said he had not. Although not hearing from my mother was painful, I found comfort in knowing she was safe. I held on to the hope that she would someday find us and we would be united again.

Batterers may abduct their children as a way of retaliating against their former spouses or partners. In more than half of the kidnappings of children by parents in the USA, the abductions occur in the context of domestic violence. In most cases, parents who are searching for their children abducted by the other parent, are white females, have reported a history of domestic violence, and are the custodial parent.[4]

4　　　　Geoffrey Greif and Rebecca Hegar, "When Parents Kidnap: The Families Behind the Headlines", 272, 1992.

When my Dad enrolled us in school, he left strict orders at school indicating we were not to see or talk with our Mom. Dad and Jane made it seem like Mom was an unfit mother. He made himself out to be a superhero single parent father and my mother was made to look like a villain. To anyone who would listen, Dad pled his case as the one wronged, and my mom as an irresponsible woman who'd run off with another man and abandoned her children in the process. Never once did I hear Dad speak to others or us about how he had severely abused my mother.

Dad had filed for divorce in September 1975; however, it took time to complete the divorce proceedings. Nearly eight months went by and the divorce proceedings were coming to a close when Family Court Judge Susanne C. Sedgwick ordered Dad to release our whereabouts to the court system and Mom's attorney. Dad was ordered to call Mom at certain timeframes with us present. Up until the orders were released from the judge, Lorenzo and I had not spoken to our mother from the day we were snatched on Hanover Street.

When I finally spoke to my Mom, I was so elated. While I was on the phone with her, my Dad stayed in the room and listened to every word. It made me feel uncomfortable the way he patrolled and controlled us like a gatekeeper, while we talked with our mother. He listened as much as he could. Sometimes he would go into the other room and listen to the whole conversation on the extension phone. Other times, he would stand over me whispering to me how to respond to my Mom's questions. Our conversations were always censored, but nothing my Dad did mattered to me anymore. The only thing that mattered was that I was able to talk to her, hear her voice, and know she was alive and safe. Nothing else mattered to me. Each conversation with her always resulted in a glimmer of hope that we would someday be together again.

Once when I was talking to my Mom, I didn't want our conversation to end. I wanted to keep talking to her but my Dad signaled our scheduled time was over and gestured we had to get off the telephone. I told my Mom I wanted to keep talking and had more things to tell her. Mom suggested that we could write to each other. This turned out to be one of the greatest gifts of my childhood.

In the beginning, Dad complied with the courts. But after awhile, he secretly rebelled and ignored the court order. He didn't allow us to call our Mom on a regular basis. He lied and told Judge Sedgwick that he had. At first, the judge believed him when he said he'd complied, but eventually she became suspicious and issued him a stern warning. Judge Sedgwick forcefully stated that if we missed a single conference call, she would have him thrown in jail for contempt of court. Tentatively, Dad conformed to Judge Sedgwick's orders.

The phone calls were very important, but letters to and from my Mom made me ecstatic. What I was forbidden to communicate to her by phone, I could put in a letter. It was our own secret world. In my letters, there were no restrictions. I said whatever I wanted to say without fear of repercussions. Written words were the only avenue where I could express myself freely.

When I received a letter from Mom, I would read it over and over again. At night, sometimes I would tuck her most recent letter in my pillow. I saved her letters hidden in my dresser drawer. On days when it seemed like her absence overwhelmed me, I would either start writing her a letter, or read her previous letters, or both. My Mom would send me pre-addressed, stamped envelopes. In the beginning, I would write her a letter, seal it and give it to my Dad to mail. In one of our phone calls, Mom told me to look for a blue post office mail box. It wasn't long before I discovered there was a mail box one block away from our apartment building. It was across the street from my elementary school. After that, independently I would drop my letters in the mail box myself. Not surprisingly, the letters I received back from my Mom were often opened, read by my Dad, and resealed.

Teacher evaluations were part of the divorce and custody proceedings. Dad appeared as the model parent to our teachers. I can remember one time my Dad met with my second grade teacher, Mrs. Gertrude. She was an older woman with gray hair. She was heavy-set and mean. She had the quietest second grade class in the school. If kids were bad or talked too much in her class, she made them hold out their hands, then she would whack them with her long wooden ruler. I was instinctively an obedient child. I followed the rules and was never whacked by her ruler.

At that conference, my Dad lied so much about my Mom that I felt embarrassed and ashamed. He told Mrs. Gertrude my mother had abandoned us and did not want us. I sat there and listened as he made himself out to be the victim. I wanted so badly to tell Mrs. Gertrude the truth. In my mind I imagined how I would tell her, the words I would use, etc. I would tell her that my Dad had beaten my Mom a lot. I would tell her how sometimes he would suddenly slap or punch my Mom for no reason. He would say she had a smirk on her face or that she was laughing at him. Sometimes he thought she was ignoring him, when she was just simply contemplating how she was going to respond to him.

I wanted to defend my mother. I wanted to explain that we were only left behind because Mom was afraid. I wanted to say, "Mom had to either run for her life or risk being killed." I wanted to tell her that sometimes we had to hide from my Dad. Leaving us was the hardest thing my Mom had ever done. She wanted to take us with her but she didn't know where she was going to go. I wanted to say, "My Mom is probably looking for us right now." But I knew I couldn't say anything.

Saddened deeply, my mind was ushered back into reality. I sensed Mrs. Gertrude believed every word Dad said. Dad was so persuasive, powerful, and influential. He had Mrs. Gertrude eating out of his hands by the time we left the meeting. When he proclaimed how Mom did not want us, Mrs. Gertrude believed Dad. She was so convinced by Dad that I knew she would never be a safe person for me to talk to. I feared if I ever told her Dad was lying, she would not believe me and she would tell my father what I had said. I watched and listened as they talked. It was obvious to me Dad had won her over.

Mrs. Gertrude never asked me how I was doing or how I felt about the situation. I never told her we were really in hiding, being held as hostages against our own wills. I could not tell her that Dad had snatched us off the street and I had run away from him. I feared my Dad's violent temper too much for that.

The same night of my teacher's conference, my Dad also met with Lorenzo's fourth grade teacher, Mr. Murphy. Mr. Murphy was the most handsome teacher in the school. He was one of the few African-American male teachers. He wore the best-smelling cologne every day. He was sporty, cool, and fun. I had a secret crush on him. So did all the other girls in the school. Dad gave Mr. Murphy the same song and dance he gave to Mrs. Gertrude. He bought Dad's story, too. Like a fish caught on a hook, Dad reeled him in.

Coached and prepared by my Dad's shrewd attorney, Charles H. Williams Jr., both Mrs. Gertrude and Mr. Murphy testified to the judge that Lorenzo and I were well adjusted and well acclimated. Dad was bent on winning custody of us. To me it was all part of the ploy to force my Mom to return to him. Attorney Williams came with a high price tag, but Dad was more than willing to pay any price. The stage was set. All the actors were in place and they had rehearsed their lines.

Our parents' divorce was finalized in April of 1976. Dad was awarded physical custody of us. Mom was to receive visitation rights which included us being with her every other Christmas and every summer.

Unfortunately, when Judge Sedgwick awarded Dad custody in the divorce proceeding she stated her reasoning was due to abandonment. She indicated that because Mother had left us for more than fifteen minutes, it was viewed as abandonment by the judicial system. The fact that Mom was physically, mentally, verbally, and emotionally abused was not considered as a factor when custody was determined. No one from the judicial system ever spoke with Lorenzo or me. We were hoping and believing for the chance to speak to Judge Sedgwick. Mom had requested this on our behalf, but my Dad's attorney persuaded Judge Sedgwick it would be too traumatic for us, because we were too young to choose one parent over the other. Lorenzo and I were again left without a voice.

In my opinion, wife assault should be considered a major factor in child custody cases, as the effects on mothers and children are so serious.[5]

I remember how excited my Dad was when he came to Jane's apartment to give us the news. I was outside waiting for Lorenzo to bring my bike outside so I could ride. My Dad pulled up and jumped out of the car shouting, "I won! You guys are gonna live with me for good!" I couldn't pretend to be happy. I literally felt like I had died at that moment. From everything Mom had told us and all the kids I knew, children belonged

---

5   Zorza, J. (1995). How abused women can use the law to help protect their children. In Peled, E., Jaffe, P.G., & Edleson, J.L. (Eds.), Ending the cycle of violence: Community responses to children of battered women. Thousand Oaks, CA: Sage Publications.

and lived with their mother. I was devastated and unprepared for the news.

"You don't look happy, Nissi."

Then it hit me. I couldn't risk making him angry so as quickly as I could, I did my best to muster up my clown smile and said, "I'm happy." Dad ran into the apartment building to share his good news with Jane and everyone else.

Working through the visitation issues was difficult. The divorce settlement mandated that we spend summers and every other Christmas holiday with my Mom. The exchange was to take place in Chicago, which represented a half-way point between Minnesota and Missouri. My dad was not thrilled about the arrangement and tried to put a stop to it in any way he could.

Longing to be with Mother and communicate with her sparked me on a new journey. Between visits and phone calls, writing to Mom was the beginning of a new journey for us all. It was like a red thread in the midst of black, gray, and white tapestry. Corresponding through writing was something I carried forward from the time I was eight years old until I was into my twenties. Writing also became a critical component in my journey towards wholeness and healing.

Years later, when my Mom gifted me with the stack of letters I had written to her, words could not express the healing I received from just reading them. They were a priceless gift. Embracing and receiving those letters was like receiving a portion of me which was lost. Although I had hidden many memories in the black box, they were my memories. In written form, my memories were before my eyes and postmarked. No one, not even I, could deny the reality of what had taken place. The pain and disappointment I experienced was real. No one could take the pain away, nor could I continue to ignore the memories. The more I read my letters, the more real and authentic I became. It was like rediscovering myself and finding a portion of me I unconsciously never wanted to be found.

Next are several of the letters.

Childhood letters to Mom....

Postmarked May 14, 1976
Age Eight

Hi, Mother,
How are you doing? I am doing fine. I hope you are doing
fine.
The cat scratched me but it didn't hurt, not a bit.
I lost my seeds but I will find the seeds so we will still have
the garden.
How is Duke? I hope he is fine.
I love you.

This letter was written near the end of my second grade school year. As a school project, my teacher had given the class flower seeds. We were to plant them and chart the plant growth. I'd saved the seeds and told my mother about them. We both looked forward to planting them in her garden.

Lorenzo and I were so excited about spending the summer with Mom. We could hardly sit still. I kept counting down the days for the school year to end.

Everything was set. Mom had purchased our plane tickets. Our bags were packed. Dad simply needed to take us to the Minneapolis Airport. Determined to make things difficult for Mother, right before we were to leave, and without explanation, he refused to take us. Lorenzo and I were devastated and crushed by my Dad's decision. There was nothing anyone could say or do to make my Dad change his mind. He refused to let us go. We didn't get to see our Mom that summer. It was a terribly long summer. We continued to stay with Jane.

Seventy percent of men who abuse their female partners also abuse their children.[6]

---

6   Arbitrell Bowker and McFerron, On the relationship Between Wife Beating and Child Abuse", Feminist /Perspectives an Wife Abuse, Kersti Yilo and Michelle Bogard, eds. 1988

Letters to Mom....

Postmarked December 7, 1976
Age Eight

Hi Mom,
How are you doing? I hope you are doing fine. I am.
I cut out the pictures. Daddy said how are we going to get there?
Are you going to get us?
I love you Mom. Love Nesia
I can Handwriting a b c d e

The plans were once again in place for Mom to receive her visitation rights. We were scheduled to spend Christmas of 1976 with her. This letter was written prior to our visit. Mom had asked Lorenzo and me what we wanted for Christmas. I cut pictures out of the newspaper to show Mom what I wanted for Christmas and sent them to her. Lorenzo never got around to cutting his pictures out. He just told her what he wanted.

Since the divorce decree indicated the exchange would take place in Chicago, Mom and Dad mutually agreed to meet at Grandma Maeomia's house. Thankfully, Grandma Maeomia always made Dad feel welcomed. He never knew anything more than acceptance and love from her.

In preparation for the trip, I watched my Dad take more care than usual in the selection of his clothes and his appearance. He'd gotten a fresh haircut and a clean shave the day before. He put on cologne. He purchased my mother's favorite candy and nuts and had them in a bag in the car. Amazingly, after everything that had happened, he still felt he could woo my Mom back to him with her favorite gifts and kind words. These were the gift items from their younger dating years.

The exchange took place at Grandma Maeomia's house in Chicago. It was a safe place. There were always a lot of family members around Mom to support her and us. My Dad was never closer than a few feet to my Mom and they were never alone. Mom refused his gifts. After a few awkward minutes, he wished us a Merry Christmas, said goodbye and left.

After separation, many batterers use the issue of legal child custody as a means to threaten and control their former spouses.[7]

The period immediately after separation is a very high-risk period for abuse and killing of mothers. In a recent study, it was found that of 1,157 wife assault cases tracked through the Nova Scotia justice system, 24 percent of victims suffered abuse while male partners were exercising court-ordered child visitation.[8]

---

7   Taylor, R.L. The abuse of custody. B.C. Institute on Family Violence Newsletter, 3(4), 9-11.

8   Nova Scotia Law Reform Commission. (1995). From rhetoric to reality; Ending domestic violence in Nova Scotia.

Letters to Mom....

Postmarked January 29, 1977
Age Eight

Dear Mom,
How are you doing? I'm okay.
I had fun when I was with you. Christmas was fun, too.
I miss you Mom. Mom I love you a lot. I hope you love me
a lot. I'm going swimming. I love you Mom.
I love you a lot. You do not know how much I love you.
From Nesia to Mom. I love you.

We made it! We actually got to spend Christmas with our Mom. It was the first Christmas we'd spent with Mom after she had left in 1974. It was our best Christmas ever. Mom always made Christmas special.

The exchanges between Lorenzo and me going from one parent to the other were the most difficult part in exercising the court-ordered child visitation. Over the years, there were many exchanges. I dreaded the exchange. They were excruciatingly painful for all of us. Lorenzo didn't verbally express his feelings much, but sometimes he would get physically sick days prior to the exchange. There was one time he went several days without eating anything.

It took me years to grasp how difficult it was for my Mom not to have custody of us. Sometimes five or ten minutes to the time for Dad to take us back to Minneapolis, Mom would disappear. She could not stand to see us leave or say good-bye. Later, when we would talk on the telephone, I would ask her where she had been, and she'd say, she "had to go to the grocery store." I was a teenager when I finally caught on. Once Mom waited for Dad to come for us so she could ask him the "big question." When Dad arrived they sat down and talked. Mom politely asked my Dad to just let us stay with her. Dad seemed to consider the idea for a moment, but then nonchalantly replied, "No. I'm gonna take them back with me."

His response devastated my Mom. She ran into the bathroom and attempted to drink some type of cleaning fluid. Grandma Maeomia was right on Mom's heels and snatched the bottle out of her hand before she could get it into her mouth. I could hear my Mom weeping in the bathroom and Grandma Maeomia was consoling her.

"Lil, now you've done all you can do. There's nothing more you can do. You would hurt your kids more if you hurt yourself. You have to be strong for them and you."

Over and over mother said, "I just can't take it anymore. I just can't take it."

The bathroom door was closed, but I imagine Grandma Maeomia was holding my mother as she attempted to comfort her.

Nothing persuaded or moved my father from his position. He quietly ushered us out the door and into his car. Before I knew it we were on the highway headed back to Minneapolis.

Dad thought each time that Mom would return to him. He dangled us like carrots before my Mom. Consistently and persistently, Dad would attempt to persuade her to return with us. Relentlessly, he would bring gifts for her to the exchange but Mom would not accept the gifts. She would not deviate.

My Dad was unswerving. He always came back for us. Sometimes Dad wouldn't come the day he was supposed to and we would have a few extra days with Mom. In my heart I always wished and hoped he would not come back for us.

At the exchange I thought of the next time I would see my mother again. Thinking of the next time we would see her gave me hope. It was something I looked forward to. I would count the days, weeks, and months between visits. All the while, I felt so confused. It did not feel like Dad really wanted us. It felt like he just did not want us with our Mom. Somehow it felt like all of us were being punished.

To this day, I am grateful Mom stood her ground and never returned with us.

If the abuser has visitation rights, attempt to exchange at a safe place where the abuse victim has plenty of supporters such as a close family member's home or a location where there are many people around with lots of love and support.

Letters to Mom....

Postmarked February 14, 1977
Age Eight

Dear Mom, how are you doing?
I am doing ok. Tell Cookie I said "hi." How is Genny. Tell her
I said "hi."
Mom I have been thinking a lot about you. Sometimes I cry in
school.
I love you and miss you Mom. I always want you to know that I
will always love you.
I am doing good in school. I missed two days of school.
I am running out of Prell. I am running out of hair food.
Mom I love you. Mom, please come if you can on my birthday.

Genny, my Grandma Maeomia's sister, and her three kids had moved to Missouri. She and her two sons, Marvin and Lee, and her daughter, Cookie, lived with my Mom. Cookie and I played with our Barbie dolls together when we visited Mom during Christmas of 1976.

Sometimes sitting in class I would daydream about being with my Mom. I would sit at my desk and gaze into space. In my imagination I would travel off to a distant land. I would sit there and wonder how Mom was doing or what she was doing at that moment. Out of nowhere tears would well up in my eyes and stream down my face. It seemed foreign, how suddenly tears would come from out of nowhere and flow down my cheek. I would quickly gather myself and wipe away my tears. I didn't want anyone to see me cry and report it to my father.

There was a battle taking place in my mind. Mentally, I knew my Mom loved me, but at times, I did have doubts. My Dad was making the message clear that she didn't want us. She had abandoned us. She didn't love us. Unfortunately, from time to time, some of that got through to me and influenced me. I thought if my mother knew how much I loved her, she would love me back. I also felt like Dad wanted me to resent my Mom, so I never wanted Mom to doubt how much I loved her.

As a child I suffered from a sensitive scalp. I sometimes got sores and my scalp would become excessively dry and tender. For some reason,

Prell shampoo kept my scalp healthy and moist. I tried to explain this to Jane, but she didn't believe me. She wouldn't buy the special hair products I needed, so my Mom would send them in the mail. For the most part, I was responsible for washing and combing my own hair. The majority of the time I wore an afro but Jane would straighten my hair with a hot comb on special occasions.

In my heart, I longed to be united with Mom. I hoped she would visit on every holiday, especially my birthday and Christmas. I looked forward to every holiday, hoping she would appear. She never missed sending birthday cards and special gifts, but didn't return to Minnesota until I graduated from high school.

Letters to Mom....

Postmarked May 28, 1978
Age Ten

Dear Mom,
How are you doing? I am doing fine. I miss you a lot.
Only 328 days. That's a long time. You do not write to me.
I do not know what to say. So good bye.
Remember I miss you and I love you very, very, very, very, very,
very, very, very, much.
Picture of flower looks like you.

Age nine to ten represented another year of no communication. My Dad wouldn't allow us to spend the summer with our Mom either. Mom had no way of contacting us directly. We were still living with Jane; however, Mom didn't know where we were. Dad thought he could force my Mom to return.

It is imperative for the abuse victim to have unconditional love and support of family members, especially during difficult times. Thankfully, my Mom had all the support she needed.

In times past, my Mom had left my Dad, but he always manipulated his way back into our lives. Sometimes, leaving the abuser is a process and does not happen overnight. If you know someone in an abusive relationship and they are attempting to leave, provide them with unconditional love and support. Most likely, they will leave the abuser and return to them quite often. In some situations, it takes time to build up enough courage and self-esteem to leave the abuser for good. It's possible that each time they leave the abuser they build up more and more strength.

Without the support of family and friends, my Mom in all likelihood would have returned to my Dad.

Over 50 percent of battered women stay with the abuser because they feel they cannot support themselves and their children alone. [9]

---

9   The Women's Safe House, http://www.twsh.org/Services.html (accessed November 29, 2008).

The best case scenario is for the victim to not have any contact with the abuser. It is easier to break the cycle of abuse if there is none to VERY limited contact. With children involved it is very difficult because the victim usually has to have some contact with the abuser due to the children.

I was extremely upset and worried about my mother when I wrote this letter. At the time, I hadn't had any letters from her in nearly a year. It was unlike her to not write to me. I sensed something was wrong.

Shortly after writing this letter, I figured out why I hadn't received any letters from my Mom. Lorenzo was out riding bikes with some neighborhood kids. Jane and my Dad were in the kitchen laughing and joking around. They didn't know I was in my room playing quietly. I heard my father say, "I got another letter from Lil to Nissi." They snickered as they ripped open my letter. My Dad read the letter out loud. My ears perked up and I listened. Thankfully, they read it out loud.

Summer of 1978
Age Ten

Dear Nissi,

I just got your letter. I do not understand. I have been writing to you. Did you get my letters?

Everything is fine. I am doing well. I miss you guys so much.

I have been trying to reach you guys by telephone, but whenever I call your Dad says you guys are not at home.

I love you and cannot wait to see you.

I was relieved. Nothing else mattered any more. I was on cloud nine. I felt like God himself answered the cry that was within me. I also knew Dad was keeping Mom's letters from me. I never said anything to my father or to Jane. Nothing they did or didn't do mattered. My Mom was safe and she still loved me.

I left my toys out on the floor, slipped into the bed, and pretended to take a nap. God's grace covered me. Dad and Jane never knew I was in the apartment. After talking for a while, they left the apartment and headed to the grocery store. Once they were gone, I slipped back out of bed, put my toys back in the box and went outside to play.

Outside, I ran and ran like never before. I felt free. It was freeing to know Mom was safe. It was freeing to know Mom had been trying to reach me. My Dad just did not want her to stay in contact with us.

It wasn't very long after this incident that my father and Jane got into a huge argument. They did not speak again for almost a year. Lorenzo and I had to leave Jane's apartment and move in with my father. He lived at 3341 Second Avenue South, just about five miles from where Lorenzo and I had lived with Jane for nearly three years. We had never known where my father lived.

Letters to Mom....

Postmarked November 27, 1979
Age 11

Dear Mother,
How are you doing? I am doing ok.
I got my report card Monday. I got all S.
Mom in school we have been doing a lot of things on maps. I know Missouri's capital. The Missouri capital is Jefferson City. The abbreviation for Missouri is MO.
I know my first ten presidents. I am working on the rest of them.
Mom why don't you call us? You make me think something is wrong.
Mom I miss you so much.
We were going to come there for Christmas but Daddy changed his mind.
Please write soon. I love you.

I was in the sixth grade and Lorenzo was in the eighth grade. We were still living with my Dad. I can sense by the tone of this letter I was angry, afraid, and anxious. This was a pivotal time for me because I began to express my frustrations. I could no longer suppress my feelings of disappointment, anger, and frustration. Both Lorenzo and I were older and equally frustrated. We began to openly discuss our resentment of Dad to one another. The way he treated us was not fair or right. Occasionally, we told Mom how we felt, but because Dad was still pretty volatile, we never expressed our feelings to our father.

Doing well in school was important to both my parents, so it was important for me to give a status to Mom. Since my Dad could barely read and write, he emphasized getting an education to us all the time. Due to our circumstance, Mom really worried that our grades would suffer, so I gave her a status report on our grades as often as I could. In this letter I was letting her know my grades were fine. Lorenzo did not do as well academically so I did not mention his results. I did not want to get her upset. Lorenzo struggled academically. He was a smart student; however, he did not like to put forth much effort. He never brought a book home or did his homework as far as I know. I was much more diligent in school. I always had a strong desire to please my parents. This desire governed my performance in school and everywhere else.

Once again, the lines of communication between us and our Mom were restricted. Sometimes I would receive her letters and sometimes I would not. Dad answered the telephone when he was at home. When he was away from home, we were not allowed to answer the telephone. We had a special code for when Dad was trying to reach us by telephone. If he wanted to reach us he would let the telephone ring twice, hang up, and call right back. We'd know it was him and we were permitted to answer.

I loved to read. It was a means of escaping my painful reality. I'd sometimes envision myself as the characters. I'd often stay in my bedroom the entire weekend and read. Judy Blume was my favorite author and I read all of her books. All of her stories had happy endings and I loved stories with happy endings.

Shortly after this letter was written, I was reading in my bedroom, approximately six feet from my father's bedroom, when the phone rang. After he answered, I could tell by the change in his voice that it was Mom. He quickly pushed his door shut. But not before I heard him tell her we were not home.

That year we were scheduled to spend Christmas with Mom. My father had agreed. However, several weeks before Thanksgiving he changed his mind. While I was disappointed, over the years whether with her or not, I'd learned to just be thankful that Mom was in a good place. She was safe.

Christmas with Dad was uneventful. He would often remark, "Christmas is just another day...." And with him, it was.

CHAPTER TEN
THE DARK AGES

The years that followed were dark. It was such a time of slow deterioration and disruption I literally referred to it as the "dark ages." We lived with my father on 33rd and Second Avenue South. It was an inner city neighborhood sometimes riddled with crime, drugs, and overall dysfunction. Occasionally, Lorenzo and I had the opportunity to indulge in a dangerous lifestyle. We were able to interact with prostitutes, pimps, drug users, and drug dealers on the streets, and we sometimes saw them in our home.

While the lines of communication between us and Mom were still somewhat under Dad's control, they had improved. Dad could no longer act as the messenger and intercept the mail. The mail delivery changed from morning to late afternoon. That meant letters from my Mom arrived while my father was still at work and I was home. To his credit, my father had made more of an attempt to adhere to the visitation schedule outlined in the custody agreement. Every now and then he would get a "wild hair" and deviate from what was outlined in the custody agreement.

Unfortunately, Dad continued in the cycle of abuse during most of my growing up years. The victims were different women. While it was difficult and painful to witness or know it was taking place, it was no comparison to witnessing Mom being physically abused. The police were called to our house on more than one occasion due to the violence. Dad never went to jail though. I felt so sorry for each of Dad's girlfriends. He was not physically violent with all of them; however, he was abusive in all of his relationships. The abuse was mental, emotional, sexual and/or verbal. With each girlfriend, I hoped Dad would change. Over the years he had a number of girlfriends, and usually more than one at a time.

During my early teen years, my father developed some health issues and was off work quite a bit. There were a few times when he was off from work for extended medical leaves. During those times we were forced to rely on the welfare system for support until he was able to return to work full-time. My Dad became less and less reliable when it came to taking care of us. He led a dangerous dual lifestyle. By day he drove the city bus, and by night he used and sold drugs. Sometimes he used pills to get up and pills to go to bed. We always had plenty of alcohol and marijuana in the house. And then there was the forbidden... cocaine. Dad attempted to medicate his pain and loneliness with unhealthy relationships, drugs, and alcohol.

By the time I became a sophomore in high school, Dad had lost his job as a city bus driver due to excessive tardiness. Our financial condition really plummeted. We had to get back on welfare and our circumstances just continued to spiral downward. Dad had quickly moved into the position of a full-time drug user.

While the times were mostly dark, there were a few bright moments. The more dysfunctional our lives became, the more I strove to prove to myself and the world that I had value. I wanted desperately to be what I considered normal. Without too much effort, I excelled academically in high school. My teachers and counselors favored me. I was the model student and athlete. I thank God for the support of good teachers and counselors because in many ways they became my extended family. Unknowingly, they provided me with the support and encouragement to pursue a better life.

From the time I was sixteen years of age, I worked part-time, played sports, and participated in many extracurricular activities at school. I was blessed with God-given talent and lettered in each sport I played. My favorite sports were basketball and track. One of my proudest moments in high school came when I was chosen to represent my high school as an American-Israel Youth Ambassador. I was one out of seven students from the state of Minnesota to be selected for this opportunity. I traveled to Israel along with approximately fifty other students from across the United States to tour Israel, and meet with other students and government officials.

During my senior year in high school, I was selected as co-captain of my basketball and track team. I was voted the runner-up to class president. But the highlight of my life was to be awarded a full five-year athletic scholarship to play basketball at Creighton University in Omaha, Nebraska.

The day of my high school graduation was joyous because it represented a crossing over. It was the start of the next chapter of a whole new life. And it couldn't have come soon enough for me. I was so elated to leave home.

College Years

I began college with two main goals: to finish college and never to return home again. It would be okay to visit, but not stay or even spend the night. I had seen enough chaos and dysfunction for a lifetime. When I walked out the door, my intention was to never look back and never to return again. I wanted to say goodbye to insanity and abuse forever.

My collegiate years were some of the best years of my life. It was a time when I could leave the past behind. I was able to start a new life, a fresh life. As a student athlete, I got the opportunity to travel all across the United States. I was self-sufficient. I supported myself by working during the summer. I worked two jobs: one full-time and one part-time. I worked at Dayton's Department Store in Minneapolis, basketball camps, Greater Minneapolis and Greater Omaha Girl Scout Council, as well as the Minneapolis Legal Aid Society. With the retailer, I sold men's and women's clothing. With the Scouts, I led inner city Girl Scout troops in subsidized housing projects. I took girls ranging in age from five to twelve on field trips to the zoo and picnics, and also swimming. I enjoyed working with the girls, especially on arts and crafts projects. We often had detailed discussions about self-esteem and the importance of education. As a Legal Aid intern, I accompanied attorneys to court, ran errands, and conducted intake interviews for potential clients.

My junior year in college, I was chosen as co-captain of our Lady Jay basketball team. I graduated from college in May, 1991 with a degree in journalism. I returned to Minneapolis and found employment in the retail, banking, and insurance industries.

Meeting Peter

In March of 1992 I met Peter. I had just left a job interview for a position at a local bank and was standing at a bus stop in downtown

Minneapolis. It was freezing cold. I was standing in an enclosed heated area. Peter entered the same area. He drew my attention immediately. He was tall, dark, and handsome. There was an energy and excitement about him that drew me in. Smiling and rubbing his gloved hands together he said, "Hello." I responded with a cordial, but not warm smile. While he had potential, meeting a man at a bus stop just wasn't my idea of a romantic encounter.

But Peter wasn't put off. He began to make small talk, asking the typical questions. "Are you from around here? Where did you go to high school? Where do you go to church?" While I responded with a professional smile, my gestures were cold and distant. As we briefly talked, I learned we both had grown up blocks from one another. We had many of the same hobbies. Both of us attended church regularly and enjoyed sports. It felt strange because we had never met before. Yet, when I looked at him it felt like I had already met him or knew him from somewhere else.

Again, the bus stop was not a place I wanted to meet someone. So, I politely finished the conversation. Peter caught the drift and said, "It was nice meeting you." He passed through the city bus terminal and proceeded into the next building. My bus finally arrived and I went on my merry way.

Several weeks later we nearly bumped into each other a second time. We were both shopping at a local retail store. Peter made small talk again. This time I was warmer. He invited me to lunch since we both worked downtown. We exchanged telephone numbers and that was the beginning of a beautiful friendship.

Peter and I would talk on the phone for hours. We started dating. We fell in love. After dating six months he asked me to marry him. I gave him an enthusiastic "yes" and we started marriage counseling sessions with the assistant pastor of our local church. Two months after that, my life took a brand new course when Peter and I were married.

"Love is blind. Marriage is an eye opener!!"
Author Unknown

Chapter Eleven
As a Child, Family
Violence Impacted Me

In reflecting back, I can see where witnessing family violence had a profound impact on me as a child. It is my opinion that witnessing family violence can be equally as crippling as living in a home where a child is being physically abused or living with a parent who struggles with an addiction. Instability, neglect, and physical and emotional abandonment are just a few of the common traits that come to my mind in an environment where family violence, child abuse, or addiction is taking place within the household. Witnessing domestic violence impacts our emotional, mental, spiritual, and physical state of being.

In the earlier chapters, I shared with you how family violence impacted my memories and emotions and was the catalyst for me developing the internal black box. Now I would like to share how it impacted me in other facets.

As a child, one of the ways I attempted to cope with family violence was that I would constantly emotionally abandon myself. Abandoning me meant pretending or suppressing my authentic self. I could then move from the role of needing protection, – a need of mine which was going unmet, – to a place of being a protector. It meant denying my own thoughts, feelings, ideas, needs, and emotions.

While I lived in constant fear and anxiety, these were feelings I suppressed even though consciously and unconsciously I was thinking and internally worrying about what was going to happen next. "Was Dad going to show up? Who would show up – Dad, monster, Dr. Jekyll or Mr. Hyde?" Constantly I felt like I had to stay on guard to protect myself and Mom. I was fearful of my father but would not allow my fears to surface. Sometimes, I would not play outside or with other kids for fear of Dad coming home unexpectedly. I felt I needed to be prepared for the unexpected.

The fear I had of my Dad carried over to fun times, too. I can remember one time he took my brother and I to the movies. I was no older than five. We were enjoying the movie, which was Shaft. We ate a lot of popcorn and drank lots of soda. So, halfway into the movie, I needed to go to the bathroom, but Dad was so engrossed in the movie, that I was too afraid to tell him. I wanted to tell him so bad but was too afraid he would be angry with me.

I had never urinated on myself before. I knew other kids my age did, but I thought it was gross and disgusting. But this day I did. I can remember being in the theater and contemplating telling him. I was just too afraid to tell him. He was too unpredictable and I had no idea how he would respond. Rather than take a chance he might get upset, I just decided I would urinate on myself, hoping I would not disturb his world. After the movie he realized what I had done.

Peeing on myself was traumatic for me because I felt I needed to abandon one of my basic needs to accommodate and avoid dealing with the monster. This was a pattern for me. I would abandon myself on a regular basis to avoid dealing with the monster or to protect Mom. In protecting Mom I made myself vulnerable to the monster by standing up when I was afraid, too. I became a circus clown in the ring used to distract the lion long enough for the ringmaster to have a chance to get away.

Another way I abandoned myself or hid within myself was in one of my personality traits. I have a need to have things together, look polished, and be poised at all times. From a very early age that was me. I learned how to keep it together and look together, even if I was living in pure chaos. No one would have ever guessed my home life was extremely dysfunctional, because I was keeping things together and looking together. It was part of my personality and also one of my weapons stored in my arsenal.

Perfection was a weapon I used to cope with dysfunction. The more dysfunctional things were, the more extreme I became in keeping it together. This was manifested at a level far beyond what was appropriate for my age, and that's where the difference lies. What was appropriate for a kid at my age level? I went well beyond that. I was the kind of kid that did not like to get dirty. In fact, I hated being dirty. I wanted everything to look good and orderly. It was my internal attempt to control the uncontrollable. As long as I had some resemblance of order, it kept me from having to face reality and true circumstances.

Playing, being a normal child, or acting childish was difficult for me. When I played it was usually with kids older than me and our activities were adult-like activities. For example, cooking with an Easy Bake oven, playing house where I was the mother, vacuuming with a play or real vacuum cleaner. My childhood friends nicknamed me "Mama Nissi." Most of my play time I was acting like a mother, picking up after others and keeping everything in order and taking care of the other kids. Sometimes I would not play with other kids for fear of getting dirty. Or, if I played outside with other kids, I would change clothes multiple times during the day to look perfect. It wasn't just changing my clothes either. This meant I needed to bathe too and get clean again. I needed and wanted to stay together. I hardly ever got into trouble or needed to be disciplined. My Dad called me his princess. In my mind, I wanted to please him and so wanted to be a perfect princess.

Throughout our family violence, both my brother and I were attempting to protect ourselves and our mother in our own way. We each were left alone to process the events on our own. Lorenzo was paralyzed by fear and escaped into his mind. I was equally terrorized by fear but responded in a fight mode.

Mentally, it was difficult to concentrate in school. I was in school physically, but mentally I was not there. I can recall in vivid detail, traumatic events from witnessing family violence. However, I cannot recall either of my teachers' names or faces during the first two years of school while I was in kindergarten or first grade. I cannot recall any of my classmates' names or faces, either – not even one. When I attempt to recall the faces of my classmates or teachers from kindergarten and first grade, there is nothing there. Everyone's faces are blank. Most likely this is due to post traumatic stress from all the chaos.

During the first two years of school, much of what I learned came from Lorenzo. When he started writing, so did I. How I learned to read was almost automatic; however, the process of reading or sounding out words was foreign to me until I reached my junior year in high school.

When my Mom left I was going into the first grade. The first grade was by far the roughest year to maintain focus in school even though the family violence had stopped. Mom had always been our primary caregiver and provided us with some stability. During the first grade there was no real stability or emotional support. Not being able to contact Mom was tormenting to me as a child.

Second grade was much better because we had seen Mom and knew she was doing fine. The more I was able to communicate with Mom either verbally or in writing, the better I felt and was able to function mentally. Each year my mental state of being and mental stability became better from second grade on. I can recall my teachers' and classmates' names. In addition, I can recall activities in the classroom, playing on the playground, etc.

Spiritually, during the years Mom experienced abuse, we prayed a lot. It is a miracle she did not totally lose her mind. I credit much of this to her faith in God. I can remember us going to pray at the altar often. Mom would stay on the altar and cry out to God. Every time she went to the altar, I went right alongside her. Oh, how she would cry. It hurt me so to see my mother in so much pain and turmoil. We would stay on our knees at the altar for what seemed like a long time. I was probably around three or four years old at the time. We were still living in Chicago and attending my grandmother's church. When Mom left the altar, I left the altar. I would ask her, "Why are you crying?" She never answered this question even though I would ask her every Sunday. She would just look me in the eyes and not say a word.

Through watching my mother pray, I developed a belief in God. No matter what else happened, there was a seed planted on the inside of me assuring me of a power greater than any human being. Praying at bedtime became the foundation for my faith.

Physically, at a young age I carried my father's rage inside of me. I did not like to get angry as a child because it took me to places and depths beyond my control. When I became very angry, I became like my father, out of control and full of RAGE. I tried with everything within me to manage my anger by avoiding situations and people which made me angry.

At times, like a starving lion getting ready to devour its prey, I would become out of control with rage. There was a boy who lived next door to me who would constantly tease and aggravate me. I did my best to avoid him by keeping my distance. He frustrated me with his teasing and taunting. Sometimes, he would take something that belonged to me or pull my hair. Well, one day it happened. He either pushed or hit me and I just snapped. I turned into a monster and attacked him with a vengeance. I pulled his hair, punched, and kicked him. Also, I scratched him all over his face, neck, and every exposed area.

Within myself I was present, but it was no longer me fighting him. The demon or monster had taken residence on the inside of me. Once my anger and rage was triggered, the black box took command. The rage and anger I had seen play out in front of me so many times when I had witnessed family violence, took over. I was totally out of control and could not stop of my own accord. A number of kids came to our rescue and peeled me off of him. It was hard to breathe because I was so angry. I was crying, but at the same time, I was fighting him. Rage touched the deepest part of my emotions.

It took me awhile to calm down. My heart was racing when I went home and told my Mom what had happened. I did not like to fight. With everything within me I tried to avoid fighting. In fact, looking back over my life, I never once started a fight. I knew there was something else which dwelled on the inside of me and I did not like it when it came out.

I was home for a little while before Sammy's mom was knocking at our door to find out what had happened. My Mom protected me and explained what had transpired. I had complained to her prior to this incident how Sammy would pick on me. Although Mom did not see Sammy, she understood that I had crossed over into rage and "lost it." Unfortunately, this was not the first time I had snapped. Mom had seen the same rage on the inside of me at home. It came out when I tried to protect her. Sometimes it came out with my brother as well.

With Sammy it was very severe. When Sammy went to school the next day the teachers contacted the police. They thought he was abused by a parent or another adult due to the severity. Two police officers came out to investigate. They started at Sammy's house first. His Mom told them what had happened and directed them to our apartment.

I was playing in our bedroom when the knock came at the back door. Dad was not home from work yet. Mom was in the kitchen cooking and she went to answer the back door. I looked to see who it was and then stepped back into our bedroom when I saw it was the police. I could hear them talking about me. I stayed out of sight because I was afraid of them too. They asked Mom a number of questions. After she explained what had happened they were still very skeptical. Then finally one of the officers asked, "Ma'am, how old is your daughter?" Mom answered, "She's six years old."

"Ma'am, we would like to see her. We would like to talk to her." Mom then called for me.

I stepped around the corner and cautiously proceeded toward the door where they were still standing. I could see they were surprised as they bent over to talk to me. They were expecting an older or larger child. I was small in size, but carried a monster or demon that was much larger and stronger than a child. Mom bent down to me and asked,

"Can you tell the police officers what happened with you and Sammy? You are not in trouble; they just want to know what happened."

I explained what had happened with all sincerity. I explained how he continually teased me. They believed what I was saying, but at the same time they shook their heads in disbelief. They explained to me I was not to play with Sammy any more. They said they would talk to Sammy too, and tell him he was not to play or talk to me anymore. The police left our house and went back to Sammy's house.

I never talked to or played with Sammy again.

Chapter Twelve
As an Adult, Family
Violence Impacted Me

Like a masterpiece, it took me years to develop the denial system I had built. It was like a fortress all around me. Intuitively I had built my fortress of denial, my very own coping system which I had existed or operated from. Denial for me consisted of:

- **D**epriving self
- **E**mptiness on the inside
- **N**eedless on the surface
- **I**mperfections of others refused
- **A**uthentic self suppressed
- **L**oss of self-worth

Depriving self

While we courted, Peter was one of the nicest guys I had ever dated. He treated me like I was a princess. In my mind, he was the knight in shining armor I had always hoped to spend the rest of my life with. He was very positive, upbeat, and full of energy. He loved to explore, see new places, and meet new people. He had an incredible gift of networking. He was wonderful. When I say wonderful, I mean wonderful. He celebrated me. I had never had so much fun. We laughed a lot and he brought a new level of excitement and joy to my life.

Not once was Peter abusive toward me while we were dating. I had never even seen him get angry until after we were married.

The only sign which indicated Peter was an abuser, was that he shared with me he had been abusive in his relationships in the past. This should have been a huge STOP sign to me. It wasn't though. I did not ask any probing questions or inquire for details. When he told me that some of his past relationships were abusive, it was like I did not really hear him. I heard him, but I did not REALLY hear him. He hinted that the women had provoked him to violence. Quickly, he clarified that he was completely transformed due to his Christian experience. I believed him.

They say love is blind. I thought he would never abuse me. He just did not seem like the abusive type, I thought to myself. For me I was blind and naive. He was so nice, I continually reasoned within myself. Obviously, my denial filtering system was on. Reality was far from my reach.

Like a lobster being boiled slowly in water, I did not realize I had already stepped into a cycle of abuse by being intimately involved with an abuser. I did not reflect back on the violence I had witnessed as a child. It was so well hidden in the little black box in my mind and I did not want to go to that place of darkness. I knew in my conscious mind and could recall from memory the abuse I had witnessed. I kept the memories and thoughts related to abuse suppressed. I can remember always having an underlying thought concerning abuse, which was: "it will never happen to me."

We were married for less than thirty days when the verbal abuse started. The abuse was camouflaged. It started out with belittling. As time went on, things became worse. There were peaks and valleys. Peaks were times when everything was going well, and valleys were when mental, emotional, physical, verbal or sexual abuse was taking place. Each time something occurred, somehow I convinced myself there was hope because Peter was so remorseful.

Looking back, in some ways I still felt like the little girl longing, wishing, and believing the demon would leave Dad forever. I kept hoping that one day change was going to come, like magic, and somehow, Dad would appear and never change back. Someday, I thought, Peter would appear permanently, too.

I deprived myself of being in touch with my own thoughts, feelings, and emotions so I could remain in the abusive relationship. Oftentimes, I was completely out of touch with my own feelings and reality. Cyclically, I deprived myself of the need to feel safe and secure. I easily gave away my interests, dreams, and security. This gave me the ability to serve the cycle of family violence in whatever capacity was needed.

For example, as a child I did whatever I could to please Dad. He liked sports, so I loved sports. I knew his favorite teams and players. I followed his favorite players and gave him unsolicited reports. I knew what they scored in a game and when they were scheduled to play next. Whatever he liked or wanted to do, I went along with it. I did everything I could to make him happy. He was my father and like most little girls, I longed for his attention, love, affirmation and praise. I wanted him to spend time with me.

Another example is that Dad was unorganized. He liked having everything in order, but did not know how to find, create or obtain order. In contrast, I was a master at organization. I kept Dad organized by keeping his room clean, fixing his bed, washing, folding, and putting away his clothes. I did this when I was as young as ten years old. I even cooked, ironed Dad's clothes, and laid them out for him. This was not normal. A child would have usually been playing, watching television, or having fun.

As an adult, I deprived myself in this same manner. I married a man who I could continue my role of caretaker with. I did not have time for friends or pursing my own dreams. All my interest revolved around Peter's interests. What he liked, I loved. He really enjoyed ordering pizza and watching football, so I would sit there, eat pizza, and watch football. Even though I was concerned about gaining weight, I found joy in it because it made Peter happy. Nor did I really like to see players tackling each other. Football represented violence to me. It was painful to watch players hitting each other. Sometimes I would watch the game with my eyes closed and ears plugged.

For as long as I can remember, I wanted to write a book. I started writing letters and poems when I was eight years old. When I was in the fifth grade I received a journal from Mom on my birthday. It was one of my most prized possessions. I still have this journal today. As an adult, I had never pursued my own passion and dream of writing a book until after I stepped out of the abuse cycle. What's sad to me is I never even made an attempt to pursue my dream. Over the years I have assisted so many others in pursuing their dreams, businesses, ministries, etc.

With Peter, I tried to make life as easy as possible for him by scheduling his appointments, keeping him organized, and well put together. I had no life outside of Peter. Nearly all of our friends were friends he had made for us. I had only one friend I could call my own. There was trouble brewing and it was only a matter of time before things exploded.

Emptiness on the inside

Our first encounter with a psychologist was eye-opening for me. There Peter and I were sitting in a psychologist's office receiving marriage counseling. It was then that I came face-to-face with the demon. The veil that had masked abuse and family violence was finally lifted. When the psychologist turned to me and said, "You are in an abusive relationship," I thought to myself, "Really? Me, in an abusive relationship?" I felt naked and ashamed. I wanted so desperately to run and hide. I could no longer mask my own pain. I knew Peter had problems, but abuse? I wasn't being physically abused like I had seen Mom abused. I tried to rationalize it all in my mind as I had so many times before.

As the psychologist talked I became mentally stuck on his one statement, "You are in an abusive relationship." Then the memories began to flash back in my mind as I reflected on what had transpired in my marriage over a nine-year time span. I had suppressed my feelings and emotions for so long I could feel emptiness on the inside. The demon was exposed. I realized our nine years of marriage was riddled with abuse. I did not truly understand the depth of dysfunction I was in, until it was pointed out to me. Even though the psychologist was straightforward, my denial defense mechanism rose to the surface. I continued to think to myself... **you are in an abusive relationship!**

He continued to talk, while my heart was flooded with feelings of condemnation. "How could you let this happen? You promised yourself this would not happen." I reflected back, like snapshots on a movie screen. The black box opened and I thought of times I had to duck or dodge objects being thrown at me. Sometimes I had to leave home in a hurry or even duck from a punch being thrown at me. Somehow while the events were occurring, I was oblivious to the fact it was abuse.

I kept telling myself, "You were never hospitalized. You never had any visible physical bruises or scars. Except, maybe one time, when Peter threw his keys." We were having a heated argument; I had turned my back and walked away from Peter. Big mistake! He threw his car keys at me as hard as he could. They hit me in the back. Where he hit me hurt for weeks and I probably was bruised. But I did not look at it. I did not want to see the bruise. Nor, did I want to tell anyone. I wanted to cry and let him know how much it hurt, but I knew better. From my childhood I learned to believe that showing signs of pain meant showing signs of weakness. And, of course I was not weak. Every other time Peter broke out in a violent spell, miraculously I was able to escape, duck, or get out of his way.

My understanding of Christian faith and leaders had taught me to work through marital difficulties. The abuse I had witnessed was so much more severe than what Peter and I were going through so I rationalized in my mind that we just had problems. I would think to myself, "He did not actually hit me. I ducked in time. He swung at me, but he did not hit me. He's just frustrated and that's why he threw the telephone at me. It missed me. We can fix the hole in the wall. This is not an everyday, monthly, or quarterly occurrence. It just happens sometimes. He is a really good man, with a good heart."

As time went on food became one of my greatest comforters. I used food—especially sugar, as a way to deny and medicate my emotions and true feelings. I would go on sugar binges, consuming cakes, cookies, and candy like a monster. Sugar was my medication and kept me out of touch with my own pain and fears. As long as I self-medicated, I did not have to acknowledge what was going on. This also meant I did not have to do anything about what was taking place.

Needless on the surface

On the surface, I was needless and had everything together, just like the little girl growing up in chaos. In reality, I had become a shell of a person, only an image. I easily placed the needs and emotions of Peter above my own needs and emotions. I was more in-touch with his feelings than my own. This was familiar to me and what I had done with Mom and Dad. I was more in-touch with Mom and Dad's emotional state of being and their needs than my own. I kept my feelers out there to sense how they were feeling. It was a way to protect myself and prepare for unexpected events. Intuitively, I was sensitive to perceiving when Dad was in a bad mood or if Mom was upset. I worked hard to get Mom and Dad to laugh when I felt tension in the air. I tried to do something special for them, like make little cards, or help them with chores any way I could.

I was equally or even more sensitive to Peter's emotions. I could sense his mood and perceive when abuse might occur. When I perceived a potential for violence, I would look for escape routes in case things got out of control. I also would think of an excuse to go into work early or stay late. Sometimes, I would intentionally work longer hours just to avoid going home.

While I was keenly aware of how others were feeling, it was so much harder for me to get in-touch with my own emotions and feelings. If you asked me how I was feeling, it took me a while to respond. I actually had to stop and think about how I was feeling. There were no automatic or spontaneous responses. Peers and co-workers often said, "It seems like nothing upsets you. Why are you so calm all the time even though we have a lot going on? How do you remain calm when you are putting fires out all the time?" I would respond, "It is just part of my personality." But, I often wondered if it was because I grew up in what felt like a war zone. No high highs, no low lows, just mellow. Constantly I remained cool, calm, and collected.

Giving priority to the needs of others gave me the freedom to suppress my own needs and appear needless on the surface. As long as I appeared to have it all together and I could handle everyone's emotions, listen to their woes, and not deal with what was taking place on the inside of me, I could take care of everyone else and forget that I had needs.

On the surface, people may have thought my world was solid because I appeared needless and like I had it together. My world was far from orderly. Periodically, throughout my entire marriage, chaos, confusion, and turmoil plagued me as I came face-to-face with my family's demons on a different level. I learned to manage and mask the mess of our marriage. One thing had changed; now I was physically old enough to make decisions on my own and have a different life. Mentally, I was still caught in a cycle of abuse and dysfunction. In the beginning, only one friend and a few pastors really knew what was going on behind closed doors. For years, I felt too ashamed to tell my parents, plus I was afraid of how they would respond. I feared disapproval and rejection of myself and Peter. Keeping the secret and not acknowledging, owning or expressing my own needs were ways to self-protect myself.

> *I kept this hidden deep inside me, showing only the smooth polished front I had cultivated to protect myself.*

One of my greatest needs was the need to be accepted; this trumped all other needs. Underlying my needlessness was the prevailing question, "If people really knew me or what was going on would they accept me?" There was a fear of being exposed, which said if people knew how imperfect my life really was, maybe they would reject me. Maybe they would think I'm crazy. Worst of all, maybe others would think I deserved what I got all along. Therefore, I constantly hid behind my needlessness and appeared to have it all together on the surface. It was only a front though. It was just a way to hide all my pain, shame, and loneliness I had buried inside.

Imperfections of others refused

One of the most difficult things for me to come to grips with was I needed to do something different. If circumstances did not change, I needed to change. Denial which had served me well as a protector was no longer available to me. On that day with the psychologist, tears welled up in my eyes and rolled down my cheek. It was an awakening moment as he explained to me very frankly, "You have to change. Your husband may not change. You have to change."

Peter, like my Dad, was one of the nicest people you would ever want to meet most of the time. For so long I just focused on the fact that Peter was a good man. I would make all kinds of excuses for him, telling myself he did not want to hurt me. He was just upset. He was under a lot of pressure, etc. The reality was that Peter, also like my Dad, demonstrated characteristic traits similar to Dr. Jekyll and Mr. Hyde. I did not want to face the shame of acknowledging his duplex nature. Denial and pretending protected me. Instead of giving any thought to his character defects, I focused on his good qualities.

Peter was outgoing, articulate, intelligent, and a person everyone loved. He knew no strangers. Often, he would stop to assist someone stuck on the side of the road. He would pick up hitchhikers and give to those in need. Constantly he thought about being a blessing to others, and most of the time this is who he appeared as.

During the dark times when he was abusive, he was an entirely different person. His countenance darkened and he did not even look the same. His energy level seemed depleted. His voice went from loud to louder. Anger arose and he became like a force not to be reckoned with.

Throughout my fourteen years of marriage, mental, emotional and sexual abuse was more prevalent than physical abuse. Peter never physically put his hands on me. He would hurl objects at me like dishes, telephones, fruits, and small electrical appliances. Our walls and doors took the brunt of physical violence. On more than one occasion we had to have the sheetrock repaired or replaced due to Peter's outbursts of anger. More than once I was hit with an object on my way scurrying out the door. After getting hit with the keys, I learned not to turn my back to Peter. I could sense when violence was in the atmosphere. It seemed like a dark cloud had moved into the room. Usually, Peter would look at me with deep dissatisfaction before an outburst of anger.

There were other times Peter would just get upset out of the blue, when nothing seemed to be wrong. Out of nowhere he would become angry. When I got to a safe place, I would rehearse over and over in my mind what I had said. Thinking to myself, "What did I do to set him off? I must have somehow triggered him to make him angry." I would attempt to take responsibility for his imperfections or behavior, refusing to accept the fact it was not about me, but about him. Taking responsibility for his behavior was easier for me to accept because it made me feel like I had some control in an uncontrollable situation. What would have been healthy was for me to have focused on what I needed to do to take care of myself, get out of the situation, and get help. Instead, I was more concerned about Peter and what I did to provoke him, and thinking how I needed to change and be more sensitive.

On the other hand, I quickly learned to always keep my keys in the car. I tried to always know where my keys were just in case I had to leave home in a hurry. There were a couple of times when Peter actually swung at me as hard as he could with his fist. My defenses were up and I was on alert. When he swung with all his might I quickly ducked, ran out the nearest door, jumped in my car, and fled from home.

Later, Peter would always apologize and promise never to do it again. I would return home hours later, after he had apologized. These incidents were minimized in my mind. I would only think of them as isolated accidents. "Peter just had a temper and had lost control of his temper. It really was not that bad; after all, I was not hospitalized. Nor did I have a black eye or a busted lip." Today, this kind of thinking seems foolish. But, when I was living in the cycle of abuse it all made sense. I thought I could handle it because I had always escaped before things got out of control, and did not realize I was living in an out-of-control situation.

Authentic Self Suppressed

By the time I became an adult, I did not know who I was or what I really wanted. I had in many ways formed and transformed myself into being what everyone else wanted. I was in tune to the wants and needs of others, but I was out of tune with my own needs. Intuitively, like radar, I was good at perceiving the desires of other. The best way I can describe how I suppressed my authentic self is that I became what others wanted and needed. I could easily camouflage myself by acting out whatever role was needed at the time.

With my Dad, suppressing my authentic self looked like agreement. It meant doing everything Dad said, so I agreed with him even when I really wanted to disagree. Also, it translated into pretending and smiling as if I was happy. Constantly, I complied with Dad's requests. From day to day my brother and I did not know what to expect, so we developed a coded question. The question each day was, "What kind of mood is he in?" This set the tone for the day, as to whether we were supposed to be invisible -- out of sight and out of mind. On invisible days we stayed clear of Dad's line of sight and either played outside or in our rooms. On days when he was in a good mood, we could be visible.

No matter what kind of mood my father was in, we always needed to appear happy. We smiled when we really did not want to smile. We were not allowed to have less than happy emotions. I became very good at stuffing my true feelings and pretending.

As an adult, I adopted similar behavior. Reading the emotions of others dictated to me how I would respond. I would sense the moods of others and act accordingly.

When my authentic self began to awaken, I discovered that I had a true identity. I was a real person. Once I started getting in touch with my feelings, I could then tell how my authentic self was suppressed. Like peeling back an onion, I was coming to life as I stepped out of denial and into reality.

One time, I was sitting in a leadership meeting laughing and joking with the other managers. On the surface, it looked like I was having a good time, But inside, I was falling apart. I kept up the front at all costs. As I was sitting there with a smile on my face, I heard my authentic self speak within me. It said:

Ms. Mask

Oh, Ms. Mask
Oh, Ms. Mask how I would like to take you off
But, I am afraid it would take a saw and chain to pry you off
Instead, I just grin and snide in my foolish, foolish pride

Things were progressively getting worse at home. My heart and emotions were starting to unthaw. I could feel my emotions and was getting in touch with myself. I could sense where I really was mentally and emotionally. By this time I had been in therapy for awhile, working on childhood trauma. I was becoming more and more alive each day. I had begun opening up by talking to family and friends about what I was going through.

I had several other awakening moments as I realized how much I had suppressed my authentic self. It happened when I first started group therapy. I was sitting there with a group of women. Our assignment from the previous week was to make several telephone calls to each other. I had called a number of the ladies but never received a telephone call. As we talked about our week, I begin to think to myself, "I'm never coming back here; these women do not want me here. They probably called each other and talked about me."

Crazy thoughts had begun to run through my head the entire meeting. I was meditating on how stupid it was to be in therapy. Within myself I said, "This is the most stupid thing I have ever done. What's the therapist going to say next? Quack, quack. Now, everyone quack like a duck... quack, quack." The session went on as usual. The ladies talked, sharing their exercises. I was not engaged at all, as I was inside of my head. I did not really hear much of what anyone had said the entire meeting.

We had approached our time to close and everyone began checking out. It was then my turn to talk and check out. As I got ready to speak I had no idea what to say. All eyes were focused on me. I sat there and pondered. I heard a voice inside of me; my authentic self spoke out loud. I said, "Please, please, please, don't reject me." I was shocked at what came out of my mouth. As I looked at the other group members they were equally as shocked. I then began to cry uncontrollably. Deep, deep sobs came from my entire being. I could not control them. I could not put on the mask I had worn so well, while pretending I was needless. I could not stop crying.

I felt like a little girl who was crying for her life. That day I was able to feel the pain of rejection. I had felt rejected most of my life. I had felt rejected by my parents and other people. Most importantly, I felt rejected by myself. It seemed like there was an internal gauge measuring me all the time. It said, "You are not good enough. So, you must be what everyone wants you to be. Suppress who you really are so you can be accepted and what others want you to be." Those feelings had been there all of the time but they were suppressed and well hidden.

Loss of Self-Worth

As a child I proved my worth to Mom by protecting her. I exchanged her safety for my safety. I was more concerned about her than myself. I carried this pattern forward as an adult. In my close relationships it was so easy to focus on others. I focused on their safety, emotional state of being, and the list goes on and on. It seemed like it was easy for me to see the value and worth in others. However, it was difficult to see where I had inherent worth. My sense of self-worth was based solely on how well I had performed and what I could do for someone else. If I performed well, then I could see I had worth. If I performed poorly it seemed as if I had no or little value.

On the surface, my loss of self-worth served me well. It pushed me to work hard. Within my own strength I was driven to shine and perform to the best of my abilities. On the flip side, it was exhausting. It meant

I always had to be on my "A" game. There was no time for resting or relaxing.

For example, in high school I played sports, was in multiple extra-curricular activities, and worked part-time. I would have a game (basketball or soccer) on Friday nights. After the game I would get dropped off at my job working for Burger King. There I would work from 9 p.m. to 5 a.m. The next night I worked the same shift. There was no time for hanging out with friends or fooling around. I seldom went to the movies, watched television, or talked on the telephone. Everything was work and performance.

As an adult I continued this pattern, staying busy with multiple projects, taking little time for myself, and thinking I had to be there to assist others. I told myself that what they needed or had going on was more important than what I needed or felt.

Like a dark cloud hanging over me that would never dissipate, it seemed like I felt I was worth-LESS than other people. I could recognize gifts and talents in others. I looked at all Peter's great qualities and told myself he was worth the investment. He was so worth the investment that I repeatedly decided to endure, accept, and tolerate abusive behavior. I did not know I had inherent value and worth, so I consistently sold myself short, and I was constantly trying to prove to the world and myself that I had worth.

There was one time my company was in the process of relocating me to another state. The items I deemed precious and valuable in my home were ones the moving company had to pack. Each item the moving company packed was automatically insured. I had the option to take items from my office to my home for the moving company to pack my office items as well. I didn't think I needed to take all my personal things home. So, I packed the majority of them and shipped them to my new office through inner-office mail.

There were a few items which were somewhat fragile that I shipped inter-office. One of them was a glass bell. I had received the bell as a reward for a program I had graduated from. It was a nice glass bell, but I never thought much about it. So, when it came to packing, I packed the glass bell myself and sent it on with some of my other items. When the glass bell arrived to the new location it was broken. Like I said, I didn't think a whole lot of the glass bell. I figured when I got a chance I would replace it. I had given it a value of approximately $50-$75. I had decided I would not turn this in to the company as a claim. I threw the broken glass bell in the trash can.

Six months had gone by and I remembered I had not replaced the glass bell. I was feeling more settled in my new location and getting everything in order. I contacted the program I had graduated from to obtain another glass bell. They indicated they no longer awarded program completers with the glass bell; however, they could give me the company name and information that made the glass bell. I got the information and contacted the company. I explained to the gentlemen who answered the telephone what I was looking for and what program had ordered the item. He said he would need to research it and get back to me. After a few weeks the gentleman called me with the information regarding the glass bell. I nearly fell out of my chair when he told me it was going to cost $475 to replace the glass bell because it was handmade.

Then revelation came to me. I was like the glass bell. I had treated myself like I was worth-LESS. I had treated myself as if I had little to no value. Had I known my self-worth, I would have handled myself differently. Before the abuse even started I would have discontinued the courtship when I knew of Peter's violent past. Because I had no self-worth, I was willing to risk being abused. It was not until I awakened to my own self-worth that I was able to step out of the abuse cycle.

PART THREE

THE COURAGE TO FACE THE BLACK BOX—OVERCOMING THE "BLACK BOX" AND BEING IN COMMAND AS AN ADULT

Chapter Thirteen
Emptying the "Black Box"

Coming into Reality

Busy As A Bee

I am busy, busy, busy as a bee;
I will take care of everyone but me.
Oh, please, oh please just accept me.
I don't have needs or emotions. I am looking for love in
any form or notion.
Oh, please, oh please, take this pain away.
You can't make me stop or turn me away.
I have been abused before and believe it's the only way.
Comfort and familiar pain I have grown to accept.
The abuse of my lovers is the only secret I have kept.

I was standing at the kitchen sink when I heard this little song coming from within me. "I am busy, busy, busy as a bee. I will take care of everyone but me."

It was frightening to hear this. It was my inner voice speaking, attempting to get my attention. My authentic self – who I really am at the core – was speaking to my adapted self, the person whom I had become to fulfill a role or meet the needs of others. My adapted self was in command that day. My adapted self often relished fitting in and being accepted by others. The authentic side of me was being suppressed until that moment.

I had taken a day off from work to get some things done and spend time resting. The entire day had been consumed with activities for Peter. I had scheduled his appointments, made telephone calls for him, and the list went on and on. Before I realized it, the entire day had come and gone. I had done nothing for myself. Everything had centered around what Peter wanted or needed done. Midnight was crouching in on me and I was still doing work for Peter. That's when I heard the knock at my heart in the form of a song flying through my head. I realized what had happened. I immediately stopped what I was doing for Peter, so I could take care of me. I sat down with my journal. Then I penned the poem you read at the beginning of this chapter.

The rest of the night I spent time journaling. I reflected on my life, marriage, and the upcoming year. It was year fourteen of our marriage, nearly five years after sitting face-to-face with our first psychologist. By this time I was really in touch with my own needs and emotions. Five years earlier, I would not have heard my inner voice or authentic self speaking.

After journaling for awhile, I came to a conclusion – the same one I had come to so many times before -- but this time it was different because I had changed. However, my circumstances had only changed superficially. The same problems still existed in my marriage. The major difference was I could no longer hide behind denial. Reality had seeped into my peripheral vision.

During the first nine years of our marriage, as long as I did not admit it to myself or others, I could hide behind denial. I had counseled with pastors, yet I did not always reveal everything to them. I felt too ashamed to say what was really going on. Also, I was afraid of how Peter would respond to me or them if I told them everything. Secretly, I kept hoping and believing that things would get better between us. Then I would never have to tell the whole truth. More importantly, I would never have to admit the truth to myself.

With pastors I was able to hide in my denial. Most of the pastors we saw did not ask probing questions to get to the heart of the matter, some did not seem to have strong discernment, and others just were not equipped to deal with people who had been raised in extreme dysfunction. There were several pastors who did discern the dysfunction; however, Peter was not honest with them. And, of course I did not freely open my life to them because of shame, denial and lack of awareness.

I felt lonely in the process, yearning to be understood. Yet, I was afraid no one would really understand me. I also feared being rejected and judged by others. So, I kept secrets hidden deep inside of the black box. The more that I reflect back, I do not think I was even capable of articulating my life experiences without being with a trained professional. Denial had enveloped my thinking.

I firmly believe you can find freedom through receiving inner healing or deliverance from a minister who is gifted and/or trained in this area. In my experience, it was really well-trained Christian counselors, ministers, psychotherapist, and psychologists who assisted and guided me on a journey of healing and wholeness. I am neither a licensed counselor nor psychotherapist, but I have ministered inner healing and deliverance through prayer to individuals and families over the years and seen some immediate results.

In addition, I have known a number of ministers who minister through prayer and achieve miraculous results in the area of inner healing and deliverance. I have also at times seen people prayed for countless times without lasting results. It is especially during these situations I strongly recommended well-trained Christian professionals and ministers gifted in inner healing and deliverance as an avenue to receive healing and wholeness.

Some people may receive instant healing and deliverance through prayer, meditation, confession and/or having hands laid on them. Like me, there are some individuals who may have a process or journey to walk through. Trained professionals, whether it is a minister who is gifted and trained in inner healing or a counselor who has the knowledge and expertise, are a great resource. They can take people to deeper levels. Like support rails for a handicapped person, these counselors, gifted and trained ministers supported me while I moved from a place of denial to reality.

In addition, reading self-help material related to areas where I needed healing aided me in the process as well. It helped to know there were others out there like me. I was not alone and did not have to feel lonely in my DIS-ease way of living and thinking. I think of it this way: you don't know what you don't know. I would also recommend local support groups. Two of my favorite inner healing programs which can be found in many local churches are Celebrate Recovery (CR) and Restoring the Foundations (RTF). Celebrate Recovery is a fellowship of people committed to being in a safe place where people can be honest about real problems - real hurts, habits, and hang-ups - through God's love and truth. Restoring the Foundations (RTF) provides hope for healing, freedom from life's deepest struggles, and renewed purpose for living through a personal experience with God's transforming, empowering love.

Once I learned how to access the deep secret places inside of myself, the black box was no longer in command. I could go to the hidden places on my own -- the places where I could feel my own emotions and hear my inner thoughts. I was no longer desensitized to my own emotions, feelings, thoughts, and authentic self. Sometimes, intuitively I went to a deeper place. The superficial place where I had once existed from did not have the positioning it once had.

It was one thing for the black box to no longer be in command, but it was quite another thing for the black box to become empty. It was in this secret place that I was able to find healing and wholeness. In the secret place, I had to abandon denial, embrace reality, and come out of hiding. Layer by layer I had to learn techniques to dismantle and destroy the fortress of denial. The process was a journey into reality.

My journey into R-E-A-L-I-T-Y consisted of:

- **R**ecognizing the cycles and patterns in my family
- **E**xamining the cycles and patterns at work in me
- **A**cknowledging Anger
- **L**earning how to forgive from the heart
- **I**mage, restoring my self-image and developing a healthy identity
- **T**ake it or leave it; learning to accept people for where they are
- **Y**ou shall know the truth and the truth will set you free

Recognizing the cycles and patterns in my family

In the chapter, "Family Secrets Brought to Light," I go into detail about the cycles and patterns in my family. So, I will touch on that just briefly in this section. Suffice it to say that through a series of interviews and talking with family members, I learned much about our family history. The more interviews I conducted, the more I learned we had a pattern of generational family violence. It was apparent why many of my family members had become accustomed to and familiar with abuse.

Knowledge is power and ignorance is crippling. As I began to take a look at the cycles of abuse and patterns which occurred in the lives of my family members, it was eye-opening. Not only was it eye-opening; it was liberating. It was therapeutic to know that the cycles and patterns of abuse I had experienced had been in my family lineage for generations. It was invigorating because then I knew I was not the only one.

Prior to delving into my family history, I had felt so embarrassed and ashamed about being in an abusive relationship. I had constantly condemned myself and felt totally responsible for the situation I was in. I had resented and tormented myself all at the same time. Oftentimes I would rehearse in my mind all the mistakes I had made. Over and over I would play back the signs I should have seen. Frequently I would think of everything I should have done to avoid an abusive marriage.

When I realized abuse was a pattern which stemmed back at least four generations on both sides of my family, I breathed a sigh of relief. It was like an alarm went off inside of me. No wonder abuse was almost second nature, familiar, and comfortable to me in some aspects. Both my family and I had become desensitized to abuse on many levels. As I first talked to my grandparents about their parents and how they were raised, I was frightened. I could see clearly that abuse had become the norm. Abuse was prevalent throughout our families' genealogy. Our lives were twisted as each generation unknowingly continued cycles and patterns. In each generation, in some form or fashion, we carried forward patterns of abuse.

After recognizing the cycles, patterns, and demons in our family lineage, it became obvious to me how I had continued in the pattern which was set out before me. I concluded that abuse was my family's DIS-ease of choice (twisted thinking, sickness, or illness of the mind).

For me, this was the easiest step in my healing process. The next step of the process was much more painful.

Examining the cycles and patterns at work in me

In the beginning, one of my most difficult challenges was examining the cycles and patterns at work in me. I had to learn to see and recognize what was happening inside of me before I could process what was at work there. When it came to abuse, my vision was distorted and twisted.

It was easier to complete a self-examination and inventory process once I could see the cycles and patterns which had played out in the lives of my family members. I could then see clearly how I was mimicking the pattern.

I consider family abuse a DIS-ease of the mind, similar to any other dysfunctional habit. In my opinion, you can treat it in a number of ways. You can treat some sicknesses or diseases over the counter with medication. When diseases are more severe, they require medication prescribed by a medical doctor. If the disease is extreme, it may require surgery or something more invasive for its removal or healing.

With respect to abuse, I would compare over the counter medication to simply reading a book or taking anger management courses. Reading a book may give enough knowledge and awareness for some to make a change; for others, possibly suffering a difficult consequence could provoke change. For a domestic violence offender, being incarcerated could result in a change in thinking. In the case of the abuse victim, it could mean leaving everything behind to find safety.

Possibly because I witnessed family violence in my early formative years, I was a more severe or extreme case. For me, it took a five-year journey to get to the place where I could empty the black box by bringing everything into the light. The journey included prayer, reading materials, changing my environment, receiving inner healing and deliverance from ministers who were gifted in inner healing, attending support groups and getting professional help. It was difficult work to break free from abusive cycles and patterns which had become normal to me. The process of journaling aided me to first recognize, and secondly examine the cycles and patterns.

> *No matter how hard the work was, freedom was well worth the price I paid.*

> *Today, I feel like I receive dividends daily from the work I have done.*

Examining the cycles and patterns at work in me meant I needed to remain conscious of my thoughts and feelings. I had to stay in the moment and could not use my imagination to run from reality. I could no longer pretend everything was okay, when it was not okay. I had to bring root issues to my conscious mind. For example, I had to become consciously aware of when I was in pain. It meant taking inventory of my emotions and getting in touch with my feelings. I had to allow myself space to feel my feelings, and acknowledge that my feelings were real.

These were some of the cycles and patterns which I learned to identify, examine, and address when they were in operation: keeping secrets, medicating my pain, hiding, keeping a code of silence, pretending, controlling behavior, and denial. Keeping secrets meant covering up inappropriate behavior and pretending like everything was okay when it was not. By keeping secrets, no one involved in the abuse cycle had to be responsible for their own behavior and I could hide behind denial. I could then try and take sole responsibility for the situation at hand. As long as I took responsibility for a situation, it gave the illusion that I could influence the outcome. This gave me a sense of power and control over something that was obviously uncontrollable. I could also choose not to respond or take action, since it is more work to change than to let things remain the same.

Medicating my pain was a huge indicator that something was wrong. I had become a professional at self-medication. As an adult, I used sugar as a weapon against pain. Oftentimes I would consume cakes, cookies, and candy like an alcoholic would consume alcohol. I could frequently tell when I was upset or in pain because of my eating habits.

Initially, I spent much of my life hiding the "black box." The firsthand accounts of witnessing family violence were suppressed as much as possible. The demons from my past camouflaged and haunted me. They haunted me in my emotions, relationships, and belief systems. Instead of thinking rationally it was as if my mind was twisted up in knots. In many ways I was very functional, but in some areas of relationships I had a pattern of dysfunction.

Examining these patterns helped me to realize I was out of touch with reality and my authentic self. When I began the journey of finding healing and wholeness, the first step was discovery of the black box -- what had happened and what I believed. The second step was having the courage to dive deeply into the black box to determine how I was impacted and what role I had played. It was a process of acknowledging my own feelings, memories, pain, and shame. It was then and only then that I was able to begin the process of healing.

In many ways, it seemed as if I was facing my own demons. Facing past hurts and habits ultimately meant I could no longer cover up. I could no longer hide the past or pretend it never happened. No longer could I protect the abuser or victim. I could no longer keep the code of silence.

Daring to look at my past experiences and acknowledging what I had hidden, compelled me to search for a healthier perspective, identity and way of life.

For example, as a child I learned to cover up what was out of order. Covering up my pain by looking and appearing normal, and smiling when I really wanted to cry was a way I protected myself. It was easier than facing reality. Fitting in was so important to me. I thought if I could just fit in and look the part, then maybe I would be normal or functional. At bare minimum I could at least look the part, fool other people, and even deceive myself.

Sometimes I wanted to fit in so badly, I would literally have thoughts of blending into the woodwork. Sometimes, I would wish I were invisible. I would try hard to blend into the woodwork and make myself invisible. This type of behavior kept me from connecting with people or my emotions.

In regaining my sense of self, I was required to do the opposite of utilizing my old coping behaviors. For example, instead of hiding from people, I learned to connect with people. One way I learned to connect with people was to be authentic and let others see I was not really together. I began to share my own feelings. I began to open up and share things that I would have normally hidden in the past. This also meant I had to admit to myself and others that I was not perfect. In this way, I learned to embrace a new reality -- that we are all imperfect people doing the best we can.

Prior to embracing my own authenticity and imperfections, I was constantly striving for protection in perfection. My authentic self was being hidden behind a mask of togetherness. Beneath the mask were open wounds, scabs, and scars. Taking off my mask and revealing what I had been hiding was a process. Some of the most painful scars were invisible to my conscious mind. The scars of feeling rejected, abandoned, and neglected were well hidden.

I once had a friend who was on the road to healing and wholeness. Rather than embracing the process of forsaking their old coping mechanisms, they clung to them. They kept holding on to the old coping mechanisms which prevented them from coming into wholeness. One night, I had a dream about them. In this dream he had sores, scars, and scabs all over his face. The sores were in the process of healing; however, my friend kept pulling the scabs off and picking at the sores instead of just letting them heal.

In the dream I tried to stop him from pulling at the sores, and said, "No, don't do that; you are healing." But they continued to be even more diligent at pulling off their scabs. In effect, they were their own worst enemy. They were doing more damage to themselves and delaying their healing process.

In this example, we can delay our own process of healing or we can expedite the process of healing by participating with constructive behavior. I have learned that sometimes the healing process is both difficult and rewarding.

Control was another issue for me. Unconsciously, I believed a number of lies. One lie I believed was that I could be powerful and take control of an uncontrollable situation. How this had played out in my life is, sometimes I would have a difficult time walking away from people, events, and things.

Naturally, I am an optimist. I am the type of person who visualizes the glass as half full. At times, I can be overly optimistic to the degree my optimism becomes detrimental. Being overly optimistic was destructive for me when I could not accept character defects in others. My optimism was counterproductive when I would go down with a sinking ship. While the ship was sinking, my thoughts would center on how to save the ship. I always wanted to recover all, as one with a never die, never give up nature, always looking and believing for the "win-win" scenario.

In the past, I did not want to deal with the reality of limits and "win-lose" scenarios. Now, I have learned that sometimes, quitting is not always losing. Also, knowing sometimes I am quitting before I suffer greater loss.

Secondly, I believed the lie that I could protect a victim from their abuser. Growing up in the cycle of abuse, I used the defense of being a protector to the point of risking my life. Instinctively, I chose the "protector" method to survive the pain of witnessing domestic violence and at times I would hear adults talking about what had happened. All my mother's family members resented my father. They would say mean and nasty things about him to each other. When I would overhear them, I would defend my father, which made me unpopular.

Being a protector and looking out for others at my own expense, cut multiple ways. I protected my mother, father, brother, and others from the pain of reality. However, this meant I usually left myself exposed or in a situation to be abused. Mom's safety and well-being was most important to me but my Dad's image and reputation were important to me, too.

As a child, it was as if there was a little girl and super adult woman warring on the inside of me. The little girl was naive, innocent, and afraid. She believed everyone was good. For the most part the little girl remained hidden. In the same body there was a super adult woman. She was powerful and quickly moved into the position of a protector, leaving herself exposed to the world. She was afraid, too. Yet, she covered her fears very well. The super adult woman had to be responsible and make things happen. She was skeptical, could discern when people were telling the truth, and protected Mom.

Today, it is now more evident to me when the protector pattern comes to surface and wants to dominate my life. While I will probably always be a protector to some degree, I now have choices and can weigh consequences and make healthy decisions. I may not always make healthy decisions, but I now know the difference of protecting someone else at my own expense.

Self-protection was prevalent as a child and an adult. It is amazing to me when I look back, that I was aware of danger at a young age. At an early age, I learned how to maneuver through chaos and confusion well. In an effort to survive I learned to suppress my true feelings. Instinctively, I pretended like everything was fine. I forced myself to smile on the outside, even though I felt like I was dying on the inside. My true feelings were hidden deep inside myself. It was the way I chose to protect myself. Dad never realized I was constantly pretending. Consistently, I was hiding my true feelings to protect myself from the very person who was supposed to protect me.

With Dad and Peter, I feared exposing my true feelings because of the perceived potential danger. I thought sometimes my true feelings could expose me to hostility, ridicule, or interrogation. This added more shame and pain to an already painful situation.

In many ways, I worked hard to please others. I felt a need to suppress negative emotions such as disappointment and frustration. I wanted to please the world around me. Looking and appearing content seemed to have kept Dad's and Peter's temper at bay. My Dad would often say, "Put a smile on your face." And, like a puppet, a smile would appear on my face -- not an authentic smile, of course -- but, a smile which would give me room to breathe and please him.

Trust was a major factor in my relationships. If I did not fear consequences, I responded more authentically. With those who were close to me, I felt safe to be myself. For example, both my mom and Lorenzo saw a different side of me. I was able to express myself without fear to them. In my heart I knew how much my Mom and Lorenzo loved me.

As an adult, I had to learn how to reconnect with my true feelings.

When I first started talking about past pain, my voice would turn into somewhat of a child's voice.

One of my therapists even commented on this. She said, "For some reason, when you talked about what you had witnessed, it was as if I saw you turn into a little girl." In speaking up about what had happened, expressing my feelings and emotions gave me the ability to regain my voice. It allowed the little girl that seemed to still be stuck on the inside of me to grow up, mature, and experience healing.

When we are fearless about facing and exploring our past pain, I believe we can heal to the point where there's no sting left in the pain.

Acknowledging Anger

Anger was a feeling I kept deeply suppressed and hidden within the black box. I did not like getting in touch with feelings of anger. For me, anger meant a loss of control. There was no balanced or controlled or healthy anger or even emotional circuit breakers. Anger for me equated to rage.

I had seen rage firsthand and felt its power on numerous occasions. As a child and adolescent there were times I had felt rage on the inside of me. When I had crossed over into rage, I was scared of myself. I had experienced the power of rage taking over my whole body. It felt like once I got into rage, that rage possessed me. Consequently, I tried to avoid anger at all costs. If I felt or sensed myself becoming angry, I would attempt to remove myself from the situation immediately. This is how I learned to deal with my anger.

One of the steps in my emptying of the black box was getting in touch with and acknowledging the anger inside of me towards Dad. The feelings of repressed anger towards Dad surfaced independently.

At one time, my Dad had come to Colorado to live with me. His mental health issues were starting to surface. He started to struggle more and more with paranoia, fear, and anxiety. As a result, he was turning into a recluse. Sometimes he would go for days or weeks without answering his telephone. He closed himself in and became like a hermit. I was concerned about him living independently. Peter and I decided it would be best to have him come to live with us in Colorado. It worked out well at first, since we needed extra assistance in running errands, etc. It was great having him around.

One day, I was talking with my Dad on my cell phone while heading into the office to work. We were having a good conversation. We finished the conversation and before I could hang up the call, out of nowhere came the thought, "I hate him." I was taken aback by the thought that proceeded from within me. It was as if the black box had opened and seeped out a feeling which was hidden deep within. Feeling stunned by my thought, as quickly as I could, I shook it off as being a strange event. As much as possible, I discounted the thought as odd. I continued on with my day as usual.

Over a series of weeks my mind became a battleground, as negative thoughts concerning Dad increased. I was perplexed as my mind was flooded with thoughts of hatred toward him. The thoughts usually came when I was around him or had contact with him. I felt uncomfortable with my own thoughts. It was like they were my thoughts, but they were not my thoughts. I did not feel like I owned the negative thoughts which fluttered through my mind. The thought of "I hate him" began to impress upon my mind at various intervals. It wasn't a constant bombardment I felt. The thoughts were discrete.

It seemed as if the negative thoughts started out like a whisper. Over time the whisper increased to the point where it seemed to have a voice. As the voice grew stronger, I attempted to counter the negative thoughts with positive thoughts. I would tell myself over and over again, "I forgive my father. I love him. I bless him." The more the negative thoughts would come to my mind, the more I kept repeating positive statements. However, just saying and thinking the opposite was not enough to make the negative thoughts go away.

After awhile, I became fearful of harboring resentment and bitterness in my heart and soul. I started sensing the pattern of abuse in my marriage was somehow tied to my relationship with Dad. I was fearful if I did not resolve my issues with my father, I would not be able to break free from the cycle of abuse with Peter. Repeating the same pattern of abuse was a terrifying thought to me. I wanted so much more out of life. I believed, somehow, someway, there was a better life for me. I believed I could be healed from the inside out, and not just look whole, but actually be whole and healthy. The surfacing of repressed anger was a trigger for me to seek professional counseling and help, specifically related to my relationship with my Dad.

As a part of my process of healing, I did individual anger work. In addition, I worked with a psychotherapist and psychologist. I was determined to do whatever it took to change myself, and shift my thinking. I was transparent in the process. I was desperate. I got to the place where I did not hold back anything when I met with people who were trying to aid me in my process of healing and wholeness. I explained to them what was happening both in my marriage and the relationship with my father.

It was obvious my childhood issues were enmeshed with my adult issues. The more I talked about the issues, the more it became apparent the issues with my father and husband were very similar. The unresolved issues from my childhood had been carried forward.

The best part about it all is I had the power of choice, resources, and tools to work through my families' unfinished business.

Prior to that moment of discovery, the wounded side of me had been working unconsciously to bring healing and wholeness to my life. Unconsciously, I had been drawn into unhealthy relationships. Like a magnet, I kept reaching for the happy-ever-after ending to my childhood. I was searching for a conclusion or ending where my father would be Dr. Jekyll all the time.

The greatest gift in my process of healing and wholeness was that Dad was willing to join me on my journey. My father had had a metamorphous-type Christian conversion ten years prior to me starting my process of healing. He had mellowed out and become a Dad I did not have to be ashamed of. In many ways he had already become Dr. Jekyll.

Witnessing how Dad had made positive changes for himself, brought a level of healing and forgiveness to me as well. However, it was not complete. While Dad was no longer the angry, enraged man I grew up with, my demons lingered in the shadows. I carried a root of resentment and bitterness because my experience was never addressed properly. I was left incomplete.

As I met with the psychologist, she recommended that my Dad participate in the process as well. We both met with the psychologist. Openly and freely we were able to talk about what I had seen, heard, and felt as a child. There was so much freedom I experienced just talking and sharing my experience. I no longer felt the need to hide and cover up. This gave me the ability to close the chapters to my childhood trauma and unresolved issues.

Dad apologized for the wrong he had done and asked for forgiveness. He was very remorseful. It was a liberating feeling for me and him. As we talked openly, my Dad experienced freedom as well. He was also able to see how he had in some ways been conditioned to become violent by several traumatic events that had occurred in his life, the way he was raised, and wrong belief systems. As a young man, he believed being violent was part of being a man.

Once I acknowledged my anger and other underlying feelings, I was then ready to move to the next step in the process, learning to forgive.

Learning how to forgive from the heart

Learning how to forgive from the heart was a journey for me. While I had forgiven my parents in the past, after acknowledging my suppressed feelings of anger toward them, I was able to forgive them on a heart level.

For example, with regard to Dad, after discussing and exposing the anger I felt toward him, I could release the anger and past pain. There was a deeper level of healing in acknowledging my hurts, disappointments, anger, and frustrations. After we worked through issues together, I felt like a weight was lifted off my shoulders. Even though things had improved between us, this did not happen overnight; it was a process.

In the past, it seemed like my forgiveness towards Dad was more of a mental decision. But now, consciously I had made a purposeful choice to forgive Dad.

The journey towards wholeness and complete restoration regarding my relationship with Dad included us working together with a psychologist. Over several months, we periodically met one-on-one with psychologist Dr. Patricia Fancher. We also met with Dr. Fancher for joint sessions, in addition to having separate one-on-one meetings with her.

In our joint meetings we talked openly about my childhood experiences and Dad's violent episodes. Dad also was given the opportunity to openly discuss his childhood experiences with family violence. He experienced a severe degree of abuse and neglect in his childhood. It broke my heart to hear about my father's childhood experiences. Hearing what he went through helped me to understand him and have sympathy for him. In his case, I could see he was merely repeating the pattern and behavior he had once experienced as a victim of child abuse.

Talking about Dad's experience as a child was cathartic for his healing. After we addressed some of his childhood experiences, Dad was able to speak about being violent. It was much more difficult for Dad to openly discuss abuse when he was the perpetrator. Initially, he was in denial about his abusive behavior. It was hard for him to face his past demons.

We received a huge breakthrough the day I showed up for my appointment with the childhood letters Mom had saved. Reading these letters, which are included in Chapter Nine, eliminated the hidden denial for both of us. Neither Dad nor I could deny my childhood was traumatic. We were obligated to operate in reality. The letters compelled me to embrace my authentic self.

I have developed a great deal of admiration for Dad's courage to break the code of silence. As Dad recalled and discussed the abuse toward my Mom, I watched his facial expressions become distorted. His eyes would sometimes shift toward the ground as he shared. I sensed he felt ashamed of his own behavior. It seemed to be excruciatingly painful for him to recall his violent past.

After Dad shared his thoughts, feelings, and experience as an abuser, it was then my turn. Dad listened intently to me as I shared. He sat with a look of bewilderment. With tears streaming down his face he sat quietly and listened. He heard me. My voice was finally heard. I talked about past episodes of violence. I was finally able to express how terrified I felt watching him abuse Mom. To the best of my ability, I voiced my perspective on what had happened, and how painful and confusing everything had felt to me.

Based on our discussions, it was evident my father did not realize all that I was observing and processing during my formative years, while witnessing family violence. Nor did Dad realize that memories of violence would be stored in my mind like files in an old file cabinet.

Our discovery and exploratory process was uncomfortable, yet freeing. I felt the most uncomfortable with the fact that Dad's memories were less vivid than my memories. It felt bizarre how I was able to recall some of the minutest details imaginable, such as the sweat dripping from Dad's brows as he carried us down the stairs the night Mom was hospitalized, the tight and strong grip Dad had on us, And the coldness of Chicago's windy city streets as I stood watching them load Mom into the ambulance. How was I able to access some memories with such clarity and detail? Yet, I could not remember my teacher's name or any of my classmates' names until the violence and neglect had waned.

Our sessions were also freeing because it was like we were both traveling back in time to face and overcome our families' demons and the secrets we had hidden deep within our own black boxes -- the things that we never exposed to the world but rather hid from others and ourselves. In facing and openly discussing the past, we were no longer attempting to outrun our demons by denying the past.

I encourage those who have had similar family violence issues to go through a similar process. With one caveat, I strongly encourage this to be done with a licensed psychotherapist, psychologist, or professional counselor. I would not recommend doing this without a professional present. Recalling past episodes of violence can be quite traumatic and emotional for the abuse victim, witness, and perpetrator. With the support and encouragement of a professional counselor, Dad and I were able to walk through the painful memories and find healing. Through this process we were able to achieve a deeper level of emotional healing.

Along with our sessions with a psychologist, there were a number of suggested readings and exercises we both completed. Additionally, I have included Chapter 14, which consists of exercises I have found to be beneficial through my process of finding healing and wholeness.

Today, Dad and I have a good relationship. The demons of resentment, bitterness, and hatred which lurked in the shadows have totally dissipated. Now, Dad is a source of encouragement to me. Before we went through counseling together I received his encouragement through a filter. I could not really receive his encouragement in my heart. There was a guard over my heart in my relationship with him. In the back of my mind, I was always looking for the monster to show up or the other shoe to fall. Fear of him lurked in the shadows of my mind. Through the process of counseling, Dad and I both received healing from the inside out.

Getting in touch with the anger I felt toward Dad was easier than getting in touch with the resentment I felt toward Mom. The most difficult part of my journey was coming to grips with the unforgiveness and resentment I had hidden deeply within the black box. I had harbored negative emotions toward Mom too, but they were disguised.

Until I began working with a counselor, I never knew I was harboring unforgiveness and resentment toward her. They were subconsciously hidden. It was difficult to feel and admit that the victim I had tried so hard to protect, I had resentment toward. Secretly, deeply hidden within the black box, I felt like Mom owed me for leaving me behind.

The first step to me being able to forgive Mom on a deeper level was to admit I had been abandoned. After admitting I had been abandoned, I could then truly become angry about it. This released me to move another step closer to wholeness. Until I was angry, I could not move through the forgiveness cycle to achieve wholeness. Once I was angry, I could then grieve the abandonment I had experienced. My process worked like this:

- Admit I was abandoned
- Feel my anger, resentment, unforgiveness
- Grieve the losses

After I had gone through the three steps of admission, anger, and grieving I could then move forward with forgiveness. In the final step of forgiveness, I could then release Mom from the judgment I had secretly held on to in my heart. I had accused Mom in a private trial, judged her, and found her guilty. I had sentenced Mom to a lifetime of owing me for what had transpired.

Forgiveness was equal to finding wholeness.

This process involved writing a series of letters to Mom. The letters were written solely for my healing. In fact, after I finished my work with the letters I either burned them, or tied then to a balloon and released the balloon. There were a few letters I was encouraged to share in group therapy sessions.

After I had completed the series of letters, I thought I was in good shape in regard to Mom. However, later in the process Dr. Fancher gently nudged me to go deeper. She sensed there was something more.

The gentle nudge started with a suggestion. Dr. Fancher passively indicated it might be beneficial to bring my Mom in for several sessions as well. Initially, I thought to myself, "This really is not necessary. I do not have issues with Mom. She's the one I was protecting." Nevertheless, at Dr. Fancher's prompting, I mentioned it to Mom. To my surprise, Mom thought it was a good idea as well. Actually, my Mom thought it would be advantageous for both of us. An important take away from my journey of healing and wholeness is this one thing:

I could not take 100 percent confidence in my own thinking all the time.

In the process of healing, I needed to trust other people sometimes more than I trusted in my own thinking. I discovered I was powerless and helpless to some degree when it came to finding wholeness on a deep emotional level. I needed others who were looking from a different vantage point to aid me in healing. I needed other people to see my blind spots and areas where I had become weakened.

Remember, in the beginning, I thought I did not really need a psychologist, therapy, or anything. In the beginning, I believed therapy was hokey-pokey, and stupid stuff. As a member of our family, I had embraced the code of silence like it was a badge of honor. I was deceived. Our whole family was deceived into thinking we were protecting the family. In reality, we were mentally on a downward slope headed into a pit.

When I talked to Mom about going to counseling with me we were living nearly 1,000 miles from one another. She lived in Missouri at the time and I was living in Colorado. So, she came to visit me for several weeks over the summer. As we had discussed, I scheduled the meetings with Dr. Fancher.

We had individual sessions and joint sessions with Dr. Fancher. The three of us met together and talked. It was in one of our final sessions that the black box opened wide and seeped out its poisonous venom. We were at a segment in our session, where Mom was asking me to forgive her for leaving me. I needed to respond. I needed to tell Mom I forgave her. Of course I had forgiven her long before our session. I was getting ready to say the words, when I heard within my heart, "She owes me. She owes me. She owes me for leaving me. She owes me for not protecting me."

In my heart of hearts, I wanted Mom to recompense me for what had happened. Oh, it was painful. Painful to feel, and painful to know at the core of my being I did not want to forgive my Mom for having left us. On the surface, I understood why she had left me, and my brother and father. Deep within, the little girl in me never wanted to understand. She just wanted and longed to be with her mother.

My feelings of resentment and judgment towards my Mom did not surface until we were meeting with the psychologist.

In my imagination, it was like I saw a little girl in a superwoman suit that stood before Mom. She stood and said, "You owe me. You owe me for leaving me. You owe me for abandoning me." Her finger was pointed into my Mom's face, and she leaned into my Mom in an intimidating manner. Superwoman went on and said, "You must pay for what you have done. You must come back and save me. I saved you, so you now must save me. You must pay."

I had never voiced what was taking place in my imagination. Again, my first line of defense was denial. I wanted to suppress the feelings which were coming to the surface in our session. Denial gave me the ability to survive the trauma. However, denial kept me from healing and wholeness. Reality gave me the ability to find healing and wholeness.

Desperately I wanted wholeness and healing. I broke and began to weep as I came face to face with my own demons of resentment toward Mom. I cried with deep sobs. Mom wept and cried. Through Mom's tears, I sensed she deeply regretted the decision she had made the day she left. I felt she still had regrets and doubts for having left us behind. Maybe, she had not fully forgiven herself. A part of me still wanted to rescue Mom from her pain, and yet there was a side of me that wanted to hold her in a prison of resentment. The desire for my own healing outweighed the desire to hold Mom captive in judgment. Through the sobs, tears, pain, and shame I released the words from my heart. I said, "I forgive you. Mom, I forgive you."

> *Resentment is like drinking poison and expecting someone else to die.*   *Author Unknown*

It felt like another layer of shame came off as we let the past go. We were able to move forward. Under the guidance of Dr. Fancher, Mom and I role played together. In our role play, Mom came back for us. For example, in talking about the day Mom left and how abandoned I felt, Mom was able to respond. She apologized for leaving and said, "I am here for you now. I am here for you. I am here for you now." She repeated those statements over and over as she held me in her arms. I was undone at this experience. I wept like a baby in her arms. Words cannot express the experience of justice I felt. It was powerful.

I am not sure how much my mind deciphered we were role playing. Our role playing felt very real. It seemed as if we had also traveled back in time to pick up our lost treasures. In many ways it felt like I was the lost treasure. The little girl who had protected her Mom was picked up, held, comforted, and protected. Through the use of imagination and role playing, the little girl on the inside of me was no longer in a cycle of abandonment.

I believe our imagination is much more powerful than we can even imagine.

It was very powerful to role play. It felt like I was able to bring closure to episodes in my mind. As both Mom and I wept, we were able to bring closure to our past hurt and pain.

> *"Your imagination is more important than knowledge."*
> *Albert Einstein*

In reality, Mom really did come back for us; nevertheless, the memory of being left behind far outweighed the memory of when she returned. Also, Mom expressed her reasoning as to why she had left Lorenzo and me. This helped me to forgive and release her.

Until my true feelings surfaced I believe they actually held me captive to some degree. On that day in our session, I let go of the superwoman suit, and I allowed the little girl in me to be vulnerable so I could be healed.

I had always felt close to Mom. After our experience in counseling, I felt like Mom and I developed an even closer relationship. Together we were able to defeat our fears and foes by facing our family demons.

> *Like pulling a tree up by its root system, the cycle of abuse and violence was unraveled.*

I am excited to report the process of forgiveness did not stop there. It was not a once and done process. As I was writing this book something else happened. We had a surreal and spiritual experience. Usually, I talk to both my parents every weekend at a minimum. Well, one particular weekend, I had become so engrossed with writing that I did not speak with Mom. Early on that Sunday morning, I was working away. Suddenly, I felt grieved, and a deep sadness filled my heart. It felt like grief, sadness, and pain literally walked into the room as I was working. I thought I was long past the process of grieving. I was caught off guard as the thoughts inundated my mind about the struggle Mom and I went through together. The memories of me trying to protect her flooded my mind like files floating out of a file cabinet.

I saw myself as a two or three-year-old child getting in between my parents. I envisioned myself saying to my father, "Don't hit my mama." I was entangled between my parents, falling down, but getting right back up to scream, "Don't hit my mama."

Suddenly, I was swamped with the memories of us fighting, hiding, and attempting to get away from our abuser. Another level of reality was unveiled. Tears flowed from my eyes as I wept. I had never felt Mom's pain like that before. I wept as I felt our fear and anxiety. It was a heart-wrenching feeling. I experienced the loneliness of abuse in a different light.

As I sat there in tears, I allowed myself to feel and experience Mom's pain. I started coughing profusely. The coughing came from deep on the inside of my being. The best way I can describe it is, it was like the coughing was coming from my gut. I felt as though I was going to throw up or regurgitate the inside of my very being. As quickly as I could, I made my way to the bathroom. I sat on the floor and leaned over the toilet bowl. I continued to cough and spit out saliva. I felt like something flowed from my belly but there was no matter or substance to it.

Physically, I did not see anything, yet something came out of me. It was a spiritual experience. I felt exhausted but refreshed. I proceeded to wash my face. When I looked in the mirror, my skin seemed like it was brighter. I saw a light shining on my countenance. Another layer of the past came off. I went back to writing and proceeded on with my regular duties for the day.

The next morning, I was awakened by the book. I felt it was beckoning me, calling to me and wooing me to come away and write more. The book seemed like it had a voice and was calling my name. I had felt the call of this book so many times before. It was about 1:00 a.m. and I only had a few hours of sleep. Energetically, I walked back to my computer and began writing again. Around 5 a.m. I felt urged to call Mom. Mom is naturally not an early riser. She's usually never up at 5:00

a.m. I followed the guidance of my spirit to call. To my surprise, Mom was up and had been up.

As soon as Mom answered the telephone, I apologized for calling so early. I explained I felt prompted to call. We chatted for a few moments with small talk. Then I went on to tell Mom about the experience I had had. I was astonished. My mom had had a very similar experience the same day. The only difference was mine was in the morning. Mom had a similar experience in the evening. It seemed like a divine appointment with time. It was a place and time where we both received healing and freedom by just being willing to stay in the moment and feel our feelings, embracing reality.

I was able to forgive and understand Mom's dilemma on a deeper level as I experienced her hurt. I was able to have an increased degree of sympathy towards Mom. I was able to understand how painful it was for her, too, and how tormenting it must have felt to not know where we were during the years Dad had us in hiding.

It made me wonder how many times Mom had condemned herself for leaving us behind? How many times had she wished she had done something differently? How many times had Mom searched for us?

Mom and I had not talked at all on the day we had our surreal experience, and we were separated by distance. Yet, we were connected. Again, I spoke to myself and said, "I release Mom from any residue of unforgiveness, bitterness, and judgment."

I can only speculate, but I believe as I received a breakthrough it opened up a channel for my mom to receive additional inner healing as well. I assumed we had developed some type of bond due to the abuse because we suffered together.

My mom was a victim and I was a witness. I don't understand how. I cannot rationally put an explanation to what happened. The only thing I can explain is it was a supernatural experience. It was cleansing. We both felt as if a purging took place on the inside of us. We experienced a catharsis that day.

Throughout the process of my writing about our process of healing, I kept both my parents involved. Writing out our story was like peeling back layers of an onion. As each layer was pulled back we were maturing, growing, and developing healthier relationships. We were walking on a journey to wholeness together.

Image, restoring my self-image and developing a healthy identity

> I am loved.
> I am loveable.
> I am lovely.
> I am worthy of love.
> I am made in the image and likeness of God.
> I have a father in heaven who loves me unconditionally.
> I give myself permission to be happy.
> I give myself permission to be successful.
> I give myself permission to be healthy and whole.

These are words of affirmation which I often said through my process of healing and I still repeat to this day.

The exact moment it started, I am not exactly sure. All I can explain is unconsciously a faulty belief system had been constructed concerning my value and worth. Perhaps it was the result of being abandoned by both parents. Possibly it was due to the family violence I witnessed. At the core of my identity was abandonment.

The abandonment constantly spoke to me and told me I was worth-LESS. It said I had to earn value and prove my worth. Nevertheless, when I traced it back, abandonment stemmed out of our family violence issues. It was apparent to me that dealing with family violence sparked additional issues which culminated and reinforced the message I was worth-LESS. The underlying root which fueled the message which said, "I was worth-LESS," was abandonment. Admitting I was abandoned was the most difficult admission. Denial of abandonment was something I clung to for more than twenty-five years.

No one had ever asked the question until Dr. Weiss did.

Dr. Weiss asked so point blank, "Where were you when your mother left?"

"I was there."

Patiently, I sat there and waited for the next question. I had proceeded as if there was nothing to it. Dr. Weiss then said, "So you were abandoned." I became angry with him at that point for making a forbidden comment. I wondered, how he could say those words to me… "I had been abandoned."

For a moment in time, my mind relapsed back to my Dad. Dad would make the same statement. I had heard the same message so many times before. Dad would say, "Your mother does not want you; she abandoned you." I hated that statement. I resented Dad for making those same comments.

My mind slipped back into the room. Automatically, I suppressed my anger and resentment. I was a professional at suppressing negative emotions. I hid my anger toward Dad and Dr. Weiss as well. I wanted to curse at him. Instead I calmly responded, "No, she didn't leave me; she left my father. She didn't leave me." But, in reality, I had been left. I had been abandoned. I had been abandoned by both Mom and Dad.

Dr. Weiss quickly responded, "Your mother left you. You're in denial and at some point you are going to have to deal with the fact you were abandoned." Those words changed my life forever. As a child and an adult, abandonment was something unconsciously I did not want to face. Abandonment was too painful to face because it forced me to deal with underlying questions and issues. Ultimately, the difficult underlying questions were:

1. Am I loveable?
2. Am I worthy of being loved?
3. Do I have worth or value?

Based on the things I accepted in my close personal relationships, I would have had to respond with a resounding "No" to each of these questions. In my conscious mind, if you had asked me those questions, I would have shouted "Yes" to all three. Outwardly on the surface, if you had seen or met me, you would have been left with the opinion of "Yes" as well. Unfortunately, the value I placed on myself was reflected in my behavior, action, and choices in close relationships.

There was a sense of worth-LESSness (worth less than others, placing a higher value on others) which was hidden in the black box. Worth-LESSness was deeply embedded in my unconscious mind. Like a dark cloud looming over me, there was always a sense or feeling of being worth-LESS than others.

In my process of healing and recovery, I had to accept I had been abandoned and then identify with my inherent value. In identifying with my inherent value, I learned to understand that I had value and worth just because I was a human being on earth. I learned to accept that I had value without ever doing or achieving anything. It was a new discovery for me to not have to prove myself. It was a process for me to believe I had value without doing something. The faulty belief system I had developed only included earned esteem, value, and worth. Finally, I learned to accept the fact that my parents left me because they had their own set of issues. Their issues did not define me. Their issues were not my issues. Family violence was not my fault or responsibility. The things that happened were because of decisions my parents made.

Identifying with my inherent value and worth was a process. I had to intentionally become conscious of my thought life. I had to pay close attention to my own thoughts and thinking. As I began to pay close attention to my thinking, I discovered countless negative messages flowing through my mind.

One wave of thought patterns said, "That was dumb. You are dumb. How could you be so stupid?" Another thought pattern said, "Oh… you did it again. You will never get it right. You will never be together. You will always come up short. You cannot get the job done. You are not enough."

I did not realize how negative self-talk plagued my mind. It seemed as if it screamed at me at times. Some psychologists call negative thought patterns, "stinking thinking." In order to find emotional wholeness and mental stability, I had to give up "stinking thinking." For me it was a matter of life (finding wholeness) or death (staying sick). I gladly gave up the destructive habit of stinking thinking. It was work though. It did not happen overnight. I had to come to a place where I could not allow my thoughts to run wild. I had to arrest negative self-talk. I could not afford to allow negative thinking to play out inside my head.

Today, I believe we can write our own script for life with our thinking. Whether the script is good or bad is up to us. Learning, acting, and believing in this principle changed my life forever. After I started guarding my thinking, my life was never the same again. I changed from the inside out, which meant my circumstances had to change.

The second step in the process of identifying with my inherent value was to replace old messages and thoughts with new affirming messages. It was transforming for me to shift my thinking from negative thoughts to thoughts of affirmation. Thirdly, I incorporated thinking to say kind words to myself. I learned how to be gentle with myself. I got to the place where I found myself even laughing at some of my behavior, instead of thinking condemning thoughts. I started to applaud myself for just being. It felt as though I was re-wiring my brain. Guess what? My feelings followed my thoughts and words. The more I affirmed myself the better I felt about myself and life in general. As I developed a healthy belief system, I accepted my inherent value. The healthier my belief system, the better I felt and the easier it was to make good choices. It became less and less fitting and desirable to be in an intimate relationship with an abusive person.

What was I learning? I was learning how to love myself in a healthy way. I believe the first and most important love is self-love. If I had not learned to love myself, I could never give or receive healthy love. Nor would I have had the courage to leave an abusive relationship, not knowing what the future would hold for me.

Low self-esteem and worth-LESS-ness which had held me in bondage for so long was eradicated by words of affirmation. There was a noticeable change in me after thirty days of me completing this two-step process:

1. Arresting negative self-talk
2. Speaking words of affirmation

The more I practiced affirmations negative thinking and speaking lost its voice. Every now and then the negative thoughts would try to whisper to me. I could hear negative thinking murmur things like, "People don't like you. You don't fit in." However, the affirmations spoke louder than the negative whispers. What was really cool is when I got to the place where the affirmations would roll through my mind automatically.

Early on, it was a lot of effort to purposefully speak affirming words. But, when the negative thoughts came, I intentionally combated them with these words of affirmation:

- "I am worthy of love."
- "I am unique."

- "I deserve love."
- "I am loved."
- "I am precious."
- "I am valuable."
- "I am fearfully and wonderfully made."
- "I am created for mighty exploits."

As time went on, when my mind sometimes attempted to revert back and play old negative messages, I would stop the messages. The affirmation and positive messages were more powerful. I had developed the knowledge, power, and freedom to replace negative messages with positive messages.

If I had a bad day or bad experience, where I was treated less than valuable, negative thinking would revisit me. Yet, I would not allow it to stay and take up residence in my mind. If I did it would send me on a downward spiral. Instead, I would say just the opposite of what I was thinking.

For example, if I had the thought, "That was so stupid." Like turning on a recording I would tell myself:

- "I am bright."
- "I am intelligent."
- "I am kind."
- "I am witty."
- "I am creative."
- "I am resourceful."

If I could not say affirming statements out loud, I would think an affirming thought. I have found it to be very powerful to affirm myself upon awaking in the morning. It starts my day out in a positive frame of mind. Another great time is when you are getting ready for your day. Look yourself in the mirror and say words of affirmation. At night while you are drifting off to sleep is another good time, too. I try to say and think affirming thoughts as much as possible in order to reprogram my thinking.

Take it or leave it; learning to accept people for where they are

Ultimately, I had to take responsibility for myself and the choices I made. I had two choices. I could either continue to take verbal, emotional, mental, and sometimes physical abuse, or I could choose to leave the situation.

In the healing process I learned to "Take it or leave it." At the end of the day, I learned to accept people for who they are and where they are at. On a day to day basis, I learned to trust in my own intuition more than I trusted in what other people said. I learned to watch people's actions and behaviors more than their words. Believing and accepting peoples' actions more than their words is something I learned to constantly remind myself of.

In the past, growing up I had learned to trust in Dad's words more than his actions. Dad told me he loved Mom and me, but he did not always act loving toward us. I wanted to trust and believe in his words, and those of others. Through life's circumstances, I learned the hard way; actions speak louder than words.

One thing I have to remind myself of frequently is that people are not always honest. My parents taught me to always tell the truth no matter what. So, I find it sometimes hard to believe that people are dishonest. Also, I have to remind myself that people can have the best intentions in the world, and unintentionally do bad things. Sometimes, people not only lie to other people; they lie to themselves. They buy their own lies. One of my friends would always say, "A con artist always has a good story." In denial, one of the biggest lies I had bought into was that things would get better. In reality, I learned the definition of insanity was doing the same thing over and over and expecting a different result.

"Taking it or leaving it," in order to get different results meant I had to do things differently. I could have the best intentions of doing things differently; however, if I do not change my thinking, I will never make a committed, lasting change.

A change of thinking proceeded by a change of action equals committed, lasting change. I know what I really believe by what I do, not by what I say. I learned to use this as my measuring gauge in relationships with other people as well. I can know the true beliefs of others by how they respond and act. I learned to judge people by what they did, not by what they said.

People can camouflage a situation by saying the right thing. I have had acquaintances who know all the right things to say but their behavior does not align with their words. Like actors saying a line, their character or conduct does not align with what they say. They are merely doing just that -- acting or playing a role. The bottom line is, I learned to take it or leave it. Liars lie. Honest people tell the truth. When people lie it is because they are liars. There is no way around it. There is no way to sugar coat it. Abusers abuse people because they are abusive. Unless both the abuser and violence partner are willing to change, they will continue on with their behavior. Each of us has the power of choice. On the inside of each of us is the ability and power to change. We can change if we choose to change and pay the price of change.

I find that people do not change because they either consciously do not want to change, they are not ready for a change, or they are not willing to pay the price to change. Everything, I mean EVERYTHING, comes at a price. It costs to stay sick and it costs to get healed. Wholeness comes at a cost. It is a matter of which price people are willing to pay. You can stay sick and pay the price of sickness. Or you can pay the price of healing and wholeness. But each of these will come at a cost or price. One is constructive and the other destructive. One is a builder and the other is a destroyer.

In all of this I had to realize and accept that I had no control or power over others. I needed to embrace my powerlessness, understanding I was powerless to bring about change in the life of anyone other than myself.

After making peace with that understanding, the only person I could control was me. I had to accept the power of choice for me. This reality forced me to surrender magical thinking. The magical thinking I wanted to believe was that somehow, someway, I could influence the abuser. This was far from reality and kept me in the cycle of abuse. Believing I could influence the abuser gave me a sense of power and an illusion of some type of control in an uncontrollable situation. Believing I could influence the abuser was a false belief.

From a verbal and emotional perspective, I discovered another area where I had the power of choice. It was a mental choice in regard to the messages I would accept from the abuser and my own thinking. In regard to verbal abuse, the "take it or leave it" technique was critical to maintaining my own sanity. This meant when negative messages or words were spoken to me from the abuser, I had the mental ability to accept them or reject them. I learned to receive words spoken to me like receiving electronic e-mail in my inbox. Negative messages were just junk mail. I had to delete "negative messages" right away. This was done by not allowing negative words to enter my heart or play in my mind. **My mind was my space** and I developed the ability to arrest negative words and thoughts. I treated negative thoughts and words like trespassers entering onto private property.

Sometimes, when negative words were spoken to me I would have pep talks within my own mind. I learned to tell myself it wasn't really about me. For example, if I was called a b**** by Peter, I would say to myself, "That is not who I am." I would even tell myself inwardly or verbally, "I do not receive that."

Leaving an abusive relationship and/or getting to a place of mental health and strength is a process. The process of taking it or leaving it gave me the ability to gain strength until I was positioned to do something different.

In reflecting back on my childhood, "take it or leave it" was also a technique I used to survive verbal abuse from my father, until I was positioned to do something different.

Lastly, I had to accept two realities. One reality was predicated on understanding that abuse is about issues the abuser has. The abuser is usually seeking a way to feel powerful. They feel powerless and will do anything to regain power or feel powerful. Secondly, abused partners stay in an abusive pattern because of unresolved issues within themselves.

I thought about it over and over. I tried to come up with a logical explanation for abuse. No matter how hard I tried, I could never come to a point where abuse made ANY sense. So, I have learned to accept that abuse is not rational. You can never really make total sense of it. It is something that just does not make ANY sense. Therefore, I have come to this conclusion:

- Sick people do sick things
- Insane people do insane things
- Foolish people do foolish things

In contrast,

- Healthy people do healthy things
- Sane people do sane things
- Wise people do wise things

I want to leave you with one final thought; family violence perpetuates because it is a sickness and DIS-ease of the mind which dramatically impacts the entire family for generations to come if not properly dealt with.

Take it or leave it.

You shall know the truth and the truth will set you free

In the final phase of my journey toward wholeness and emptying the black box, one of the last steps included my family. As a family, the four of us met with a psychologist to discuss our history. In our meeting, I was finally able to learn the whole truth. It was freeing to ask the questions I always wondered but was too afraid to ask.

I will never forget the day we met. It was a cold winter January day in Colorado. Mom and Lorenzo had come to Colorado for our meeting and to see me speaking at a venue being held in downtown Denver. There we were. For the first time as a family Dad, Mom, Lorenzo, and I talked openly about family violence. Lorenzo and I shared candidly what we saw, heard, and felt throughout our growing up years. It was the first time Lorenzo was able to share with Dad and Mom without any reservations. I had shared with Dad and Mom in our prior meetings with the psychologist. Lorenzo and I had had a number of conversations. This time it was different because we were all present and sharing what had happened.

In our meeting as a family, what I found interesting was to hear Lorenzo's prospective. He processed things differently than I did. For example, when Mom took us from Aunt Bertha's apartment, Lorenzo felt like Mom did the same thing Dad did, while I processed it as Mom fulfilling her promise to us. My reality was different from Lorenzo's.

Each of us learned our perceived realities in our meeting. My perceived reality focused on being left behind by Mom. Being abandoned haunted me. Lorenzo and I both agreed that witnessing family violence was the worst of what we endured as children. The abandonment we experienced and being placed into hiding were very traumatic as well.

I had sometimes wondered, but only when I allowed my thinking to go to a deep place, why Mom left us. This was the question I was always too afraid to ask. I was too afraid to allow the question to escape from the black box. I was too afraid to consciously think what the answer might have been. It was much easier to avoid thinking about being left or abandoned.

After going through a process of healing which included coming out of DENIAL and facing REALITY, I finally had the courage to ask the question.

We were all sitting at the table with the psychologist, when I asked. Mom was sitting on the left side of me and Lorenzo sat on my right side. Dad sat on the other side of Lorenzo with the psychologist sitting between Mom and Dad. There was a moment of silence after Lorenzo finished talking.

The question was rolling around in my head. I turned to Mom and said, "Why did you leave us?" It was a pivotal point because it meant I was no longer afraid of Mom's answer. Growing up as a child I was unconsciously plagued with the belief I wasn't loveable or worthy of love. As a child I rationalized this with magical thinking: "she did not leave you, she left Dad." Possibly unconsciously this was my belief. Reality was too painful to accept or deal with in my conscious mind. So, my mind intuitively established a different belief or theory. My mind chose to believe she left Dad. It was less painful and more powerful to believe she left Dad. It was also easier to blame Dad.

Before Mom could respond to my question, I followed up with a second question, "Why didn't you take us, too? You took time to pack your clothes, why didn't you just take us, too?" I felt a lump in my throat and the pain on the inside of not truly knowing why. Just asking the question was therapeutic.

For a moment it seemed as though time stood still as we paused and waited for Mom to respond. Mom sat there and pondered the question for just a moment. She had known this day would come. For a moment, she paused to gather her emotions, and with tears filling her eyes, Mom began to respond. Her response came from deep within. It was apparent she had thought and asked the question of herself so many times over. She had a look on her face of deep regret. I felt her pain and I sensed her struggle. It was the same struggle she had felt the day she left.

By this time the tears had begun to stream down her face and flow like rivers. I saw sitting before me the Mom I had rescued so many times. I wanted to rescue Mom again. I wanted to take away the pain of having to respond to such a question. I felt her pain and my pain intermingled together. I too started to feel guilty for putting Mom in the position of having to answer such a question. If I could have retracted the question I probably would have done so, but it was too late. Asking the question was also something I needed to ask so I would know the truth. The truth repelled the lies I told myself.

Through her tears Mom's voice quivered as she gazed into space. Mom looked away and said, "I was afraid."

Mom broke into a sob and turned to Lorenzo and me. She said it again, "I was afraid. I did it to protect you. I was so afraid if I took you two, your father would come after us and kill us all." We wept and cried together.

Mom went on to explain that during the time when she was contemplating leaving us, there were a number of stories which appeared in the news media where the father actually killed the whole family in a rage. Mom feared it would happen to us. Mom also believed Dad would give us up to her without a fight when she returned for us.

As Mom shared, I could sense she still struggled with the decision she had made thirty years earlier. I sensed part of her pain was that she hadn't fully forgiven herself. Seeing Mom's pain and her perspective provoked an increased level of empathy in me for her. I could only slightly begin to imagine what that day was like for her, and the pain she had felt when she left us. How she must have been tormented when Dad cut off the lines of communication. Mom must have felt fearful for all of our lives.

Dad explained how badly he had wanted us to be together as a family. He was convinced Mom would return. He never thought Mom would live without us. Seeing all of our pain and trying to understand the magnitude of his decision, Dad felt very remorseful. He had never stopped to think about how his decisions impacted us all. Dad felt ashamed for what he had done and for not even taking the time to consider how we had felt.

As we recalled past events which had taken place with vivid details, Dad was awestruck. Dad could hardly remember what had happened. He could not even articulate what had happened when he responded in violence. Dad sat there listening to us in disbelief and complete terror. He was terrified by his own behavior as it was recounted to him. He was terrified we would not be able to sincerely forgive him, and terrified we wanted to hold on to the past. Dad had changed through his Christian conversion experience. It was painful for Dad to hear, believe, and accept that he had done such awful things. He listened intently. With tears streaming down his face he apologized profusely.

When the session was coming to a close and everything was out in the open, Dad again apologized. He said, "It is obvious I was insane in many respects."

I can't express it enough how much I admire Dad and Mom's courage for coming to the meeting. For listening to what each of us had to say. They both gave us a gift to hear our voices. I was especially encouraged by Dad showing up. Dad did something I am not sure most parents or abusers would be willing to do. He faced the pain of what he had done. He also owned it. Dad did not shift the blame on anyone. He simply kept saying, "I am so sorry. Can you all forgive me?"

We all cried together. We held each other. As we hugged and forgave one another, I felt like grave clothes were taken off of each of us that day. I could literally see the countenances of Dad, Mom, and Lorenzo became lighter. It was as if they had a new level of Technicolor to them.

After this experience I felt lighter within my own being. I felt like I left the meeting twenty pounds lighter. I felt free and had a newfound freedom. I was the onion which had layers upon layers peeled off.

As the psychologist began to close the session, I gazed over at Lorenzo one last time. As I looked more intently, I felt there was still some pain -- the pain which had stalked him from being abandoned. I could tell it was only the beginning of a journey for him. I longed for him to feel the same level of freedom I was feeling. We experienced the family violence together. I yearned for him to truly be free. He proceeded to ask several questions. His questions confirmed what I was feeling. This was only the beginning for him.

Lorenzo sat there and pondered the psychologist's responses to his questions. The psychologist encouraged Lorenzo to step into a process of finding healing and wholeness. Lorenzo was hesitant. He was successful as an electrician. He had loving children and a wife. He was not violent toward his wife, yet there was something missing from his life. I am hoping someday Lorenzo will complete the work we started that day. Then one day he can tell his story too.

In reflecting back, five years had passed since I began my journey to empty the black box so I could find healing and wholeness. Finally, for me I could close the chapter of family violence in my life. The dark cloud which had hovered over me for so many years had totally dissipated. I felt I was finally free.

By the end of the year I filed for a divorce from Peter. Things had not gotten any better but had become progressively worse. Peter was a good man. He just was not ready to embrace his own process of healing and wholeness. Instead, he held tightly to old coping mechanisms which were destroying him and our marriage. The divorce was granted early the following year.

I am Finally Free!

I am free.
No longer are shackles and chains holding me.
I am free.
I am free to be me.
I am free.
I am free to be all I can be.
I am free.
I am free to be me.

Chapter Fourteen
Exercises to Open the
"Black Box" and come
into Reality

Recognizing the cycles and patterns in my family

One way to research your family demons is to interview your parents, grandparents, siblings, aunts, and uncles. I found out so much by asking just a few simple questions:

- Tell what it was like when you were growing up?
- Did your parents love each other?
- How did Grandpa and Grandma meet?
- Did you witness domestic violence while you were growing up?

After you have interviewed your family members you will be prepared to answer the questions outlined below:

1.   What are the patterns which have played out in your parents' and siblings' life? Are there habits, belief systems, cycles, and patterns which are dysfunctional?

Parents/Your Siblings	***Other:***
__Emotional Abuse (Family Violence)	_____
__Sexual Abuse	_____
__Physical Abuse	_____
__Spiritual Abuse	_____
__Verbal Abuse	_____
__Alcohol Abuse	_____
__Drug Abuse	_____
__Mental Illness	_____
__Neglect	_____

2.　　What about grandparents? What are the patterns in their life? What are the good things? What are the bad things? Do you see any commonalities?

__Grandparents__	*__Other:__*
__Emotional Abuse (Family Violence)	
__Sexual Abuse	_____
__Physical Abuse	_____
__Spiritual Abuse	_____
__Verbal Abuse	_____
__Alcohol Abuse	_____
__Drug Abuse	_____
__Mental Illness	_____
__Neglect	_____

3.　　Are the relationships between your parents and their siblings functional or dysfunctional? Do you see any of the same patterns in the lives of your parents' siblings (uncles and aunts)?

__Uncles and Aunts__	*__Other:__*
__Emotional Abuse (Family Violence)	
__Sexual Abuse	_____
__Physical Abuse	_____
__Spiritual Abuse	_____
__Verbal Abuse	_____
__Alcohol Abuse	_____
__Drug Abuse	_____
__Mental Illness	_____
__Neglect	_____

Recognizing the cycles and patterns in my family

Here's a visual example of what the cycle of family violence looks like in my family.

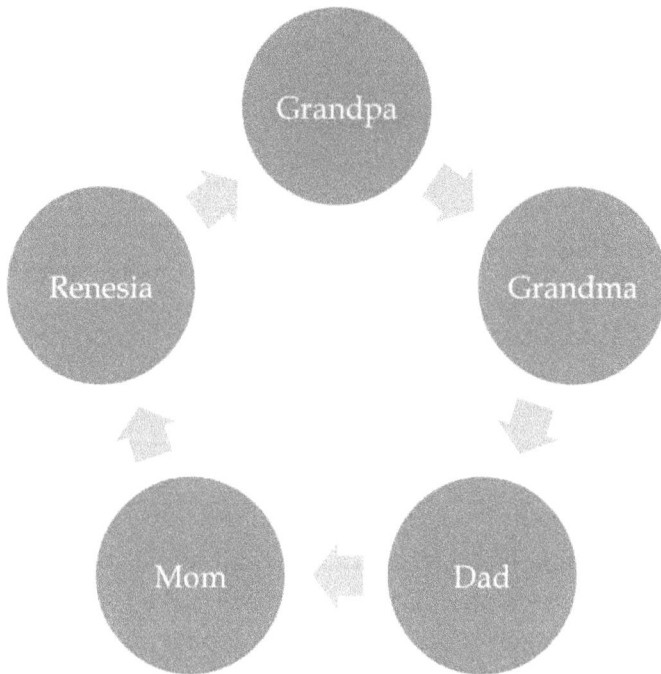

Recognizing the cycles and patterns in my family

Complete the family violence cycle for you and your family. There is no one size fits all. Your cycle may involve children or others.

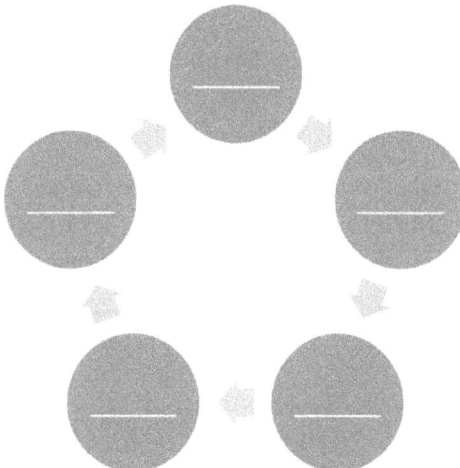

Examining the cycles and patterns at work in me

4.   Lastly, have you witnessed or experienced any of the following in your relationships? Do you see any of the same patterns between you, your parents, siblings, grandparents, uncles, and aunts?

Types of Abuses	*Other:*
__Emotional Abuse (Family Violence)	_____
__Sexual Abuse	_____
__Physical Abuse	_____
__Spiritual Abuse	_____
__Verbal Abuse	_____
__Alcohol Abuse	_____
__Drug Abuse	_____
__Mental Illness	_____
__Neglect	_____

Is witnessing family violence a pattern in your family? How many generations does it go back? Can you find one person who has struggled in this area in each generation? Are cycles or patterns a reoccurrence of dysfunction? Pay close attention to patterns. These are what I would call your family's demons.

After answering these questions, if you detect cycles and patterns which appear in current and previous generations or, if you feel caught in cyclical dysfunctional patterns, you may want to consider seeing licensed therapist, psychologist, psychotherapist, Christian counselor, self-help material, support group and/or a minister who is gifted and/or trained in the area of inner healing and deliverance.

Hopefully, this helps you to see that family violence is a family DIS-ease. Also, if you are involved in an abusive relationship, your partner most likely has a similar history of family violence. Family violence is usually generational, but not all the time.

Examining the cycles and patterns at work in me

Staying Connected through taking inventory of your emotions and feelings

In examining the cycles and patterns at work in myself, one important exercise to dismantle denial and stay connected to reality was being able to stay connected through taking inventory of my emotions. It was important for me to know what I was feeling and the circumstances surrounding my feelings.

Outlined are a number of emotions and feelings.

Staying Connected through taking inventory of your emotions and feelings

Emotions and Feelings

LOVE	ADORE
FEAR	SECURE
PAIN/HURT	JOY
SAD	HAPPY
REJECTED	ACCEPTED
ANGER	ENERGY
SHAME	GUILT
ABANDON	UPHOLD
CONTEMPT	CONTENT
LONELY	CONNECTED
HATE	LIKE

Examining the cycles and patterns at work in me

One way to take inventory of your emotions on a daily basis is to use the Emotions and Feelings Chart or any other emotional chart. I recommend journaling how you feel each day. For example,

I feel _____ when _____ .
　　　　　(put word here)　　　　　　　　(put a present situation when you feel this)

I first remember feeling _____ when _____ .
　　　　　　　　　　(put the same feeling word here)　　　　　　(explain earliest
　　　　　　　　　　　　　　　　　　　　　　　　　　　occurrence of this
　　　　　　　　　　　　　　　　　　　　　　　　　　　feeling)

Example:

I feel _____hurt_____ when ___people do not return my telephone calls___ .
　　　　　(put word here)　　　　　　　　(put a present situation when you feel this)

I first remember feeling _____hurt_____ when my Dad did not come home.
　　　　　　　　　　(put the same feeling word here)　　　　　　(explain earliest
　　　　　　　　　　　　　　　　　　　　　　　　　　　occurrence of this
　　　　　　　　　　　　　　　　　　　　　　　　　　　feeling)

Developed by Douglas Weiss, PH.D., Adapted from Intimacy

Examining the cycles and patterns at work in me

Recognizing self-abandonment

Self-abandonment was a consistent thread in which I operated. Unconsciously, I would abandon my own needs, wants, and desires to please other people. I gave priority to the needs, wants, and desires of other people. The forms of abandonment may vary from disassociating with family members to not taking care of yourself or children.

Are there any areas of your life where you have abandoned yourself due to being a witness to domestic violence or being involved in an abusive relationship? Take a look at the list below, and check off any of the abandonments that apply to you:

- ☐ Abandoning your intuition (when you knew you were right)
- ☐ Giving up significant relationships
- ☐ Giving up your own hobbies and personal interests
- ☐ Not pursuing your own personal goals
- ☐ Not pursuing an education
- ☐ Giving up your church or spirituality
- ☐ Letting how others feel take a priority in your life
- ☐ Taking care of everyone except yourself
- ☐ Not taking care of your own personal needs
- ☐ Taking on the responsibility of others' emotional needs
- ☐ Care taking
- ☐ Taking care of others to the point you abandon your own needs, safety, and emotions
- ☐ Suppressing your own desires, needs, and emotions
- ☐ Not allowing yourself goals or dreams
- ☐ Not allowing yourself to be listened to
- ☐ Not allowing yourself to have a voice or opinion
- ☐ Going along to get along
- ☐ Looking for ways to keep others at peace or happy

Examining the cycles and patterns at work in me

- ☐ Not allowing yourself to be treated with value and worth
- ☐ Not allowing yourself to be cherished, nurtured, or celebrated in a relationship
- ☐ Staying in an environment you know is not healthy for you
- ☐ Staying in an environment you know is unhealthy for your children

If you have abandoned yourself or you are living in a situation where you are in the cycle of self-abandonment, I want you to know with all of my heart, "You are worthy of love and being loved. You are worthy of living a happy and healthy life." It is up to you now to take whatever steps are necessary to get the freedom and love you deserve. You can take a step toward wholeness by sharing this with a close friend, family member, counselor, experienced minister or support group.

Developed by Douglas Weiss, PH.D., Adapted from Intimacy

Acknowledging Anger

Anger Letter

If you witnessed domestic violence or have been in an abusive relationship, you have most likely experienced some type of abandonment, neglect, or abuse. One way to rid you of anger and resentment is to write an anger letter. This letter can be written to the abuser or anyone you may be harboring anger or resentment toward due to what you witnessed or experienced.

This letter is for your healing and wholeness and should not be shared with the individual you are writing about. If fact, I really do not recommend sharing it with anyone unless it is in a therapy setting or counseling. You can make this letter as long as it needs to be and you can use any language you feel you need to use to communicate the anger you have. To find healing and wholeness, you must rid yourself of anger.

On a piece of paper, write out what you need to say.

For example:

Dear John,

I am so angry with you for yelling at me and throwing your glass at me.

Developed by Douglas Weiss, PH.D., Adapted from Intimacy

Acknowledging Anger

Read Your Letter Aloud

Take two chairs and face them directly in front of the other (front facing). You sit in one chair, directly facing the other chair. Pretend like your offender is setting in the chair directly in front of you, looking at you face to face. Now, take the letter you wrote to your offender and read it aloud.

Using our previous example, you would say, "John, I am so angry with you!"

Of course this is done with no one else around, unless you are completing this in a recovery group or therapy session. Remember, this is for your healing and wholeness. It is not to get back at the offender or for them to have any knowledge of this work being completed.

Developed by Douglas Weiss, PH.D., Adapted from Intimacy

Acknowledging Anger

<u>Get Warmed Up!</u>

It is time to get warmed up. First, get a padded baseball bat or tennis racket. Go into a bedroom or grab a pillow. If at all possible do this while you are home alone. This is your personal, private time to flush out negative emotions from your system. The goal is for you to be able to freely complete this exercise without any distractions or reservations.

After reading your letter, grab your bat. It is time to rid yourself of negative emotions. Hit the bed or pillow and symbolically let "John" have it. This is not the time to hold back, be gentle, or kind. Yell, scream, and cry but let it all out. Take whatever time you need to complete this exercise. It could take anywhere up to an hour or more to finish this exercise.

Warning: *If you have any medical conditions, consult your doctor before doing this exercise.*

Developed by Douglas Weiss, PH.D., Adapted from Intimacy

Learning how to forgive from the heart

Letting go of Guilt/Shame and Condemnation

Some domestic violence partners may have guilt, shame, or condemnation for staying in a relationship where they were being abused, or allowed their children to be abused or having exposed their children to violence. Whatever the reason is that you may have some guilt, shame, or condemnation, it is important to address it by exposing it and getting it out.

Take a piece of paper and list things that happened as a result of being a domestic violence partner which you struggle with thoughts of guilt, shame, or condemnation. Be honest with yourself.

Guilt can be defined as thinking: *"I caused the problem and I am responsible for fixing it."*

Shame can be defined as thinking: *"I am a problem; I am a mistake."*

Condemnation can be defined as thinking: *"I caused the problem, and I deserve to be punished and doomed for it."*

If you can, share your guilt/shame or remorse items from this exercise with someone who is very close to you or someone who will show you unconditional love and acceptance. It could be someone in recovery or therapy with you.

Learning how to forgive from the heart

Self-forgiveness, part II

You are often hardest on yourself. Often you may give grace and forgiveness to other people quicker than yourself. You are precious and valuable. You are worthy of receiving forgiveness. You no longer have to be trapped in guilt, shame, and remorse. You can be free.

You will need two chairs in this exercise. Sit in one chair (chair A) and place the other chair (chair B) in front of you. Sitting in chair A, imagine yourself also sitting in chair B. With your list of items you feel guilty, shame, or condemned about, ask yourself to forgive you. You can take as long as you need, and list anything else you want to forgive yourself for as well during the conversation.

When you are finished asking yourself for forgiveness, move yourself physically into chair B. In chair B, you heard a request for forgiveness. Talk to that hurting, vulnerable side of you. Be gentle. Make a decision to forgive yourself and tell her (you). This is where you can leave the past behind. Love yourself unconditionally. Love her and tell her any other nurturing things you can tell her at this time.

Now, go back to chair A. Sit and bask in the forgiveness you have received. Take deep breaths. Inhale forgiveness, and exhale unforgiveness. You may even need to open your mouth and blow out as you exhale. Imagine in your mind as you are exhaling that you are blowing out any unwanted feelings and negative, toxic emotions, i.e., unforgiveness, condemnation, self-hatred, resentment, shame, or guilt.

You can complete the forgiveness exercise regarding people in your life who have hurt you.. Pretend like an individual who has hurt you is sitting in chair B. I have found it to be liberating and freeing to complete both the anger and forgiveness exercises.

Developed by Douglas Weiss, PH.D., Adapted from Intimacy

Image, restoring my self-image and developing a healthy identity

In working on my image, I learned to build a healthy identity through affirming myself. Just because our parents did not esteem us, it does not mean we cannot esteem ourselves. If you have lost your sense of identity or know someone who has low self-esteem, I recommend using the following exercise to re-parent and rewire the brain for healthy thinking and a healthy identity.

Here's how it works. Say words of affirmation to yourself. Say them to yourself over and over. When you cannot say them out loud, think them. If you can, before you even get out of bed say at least ten affirmations. While you are brushing your teeth, look in the mirror and say or think another ten affirming statements. While you are getting dressed and ready for the day say affirming statements. Say them until they become a part of your thinking. It has been said it takes twenty-one days to form a habit. So try to take twenty-one consecutive days to say least 100 or more affirming statements to yourself daily.

Say them whether you believe them or not, your feelings will catch up! Think of your tongue and thoughts as paint being applied to canvas. You can create your own picture with the power of positive thinking and speaking.

As your day ends and you are drifting off to sleep, speak affirming statements to yourself. Say as many as you can. While lying in bed, take deep breaths, relax, and bask in the affirming statements. Meditate on affirming statements.

Be patient and consistent. Remember, you are re-arranging the pathways in your brain from putting yourself down to affirming yourself. It takes time. Catch yourself when you put yourself down and immediately give yourself an affirmation.

Pay very close attention to your thoughts during the day. For example, if you find yourself thinking, "I shouldn't have, or "I should have," notice the thought and say your affirmation. ("Should" statements are negative and limiting.)

Continue saying and thinking affirming statements until they become part of your thinking, and you are speaking them automatically. Here are a number of affirming statements you can begin with:

Image, restoring my self-image and developing a healthy identity

1. I am who God says I am

2. I am loved

3. I am accepted

4. I am kind

5. I am gentle

6. All things work together for my good

7. I have inherent value

8. I am a miracle

9. I am an original

10. There's no one else in the world like me

11. I am fearfully and wonderfully made

12. I am not a victim

13. I give myself permission to be successful

14. I have a sound mind

15. I am a victor

16. I am victorious

17. I have a life of victory

18. I have a hopeful future

19. I have a destiny

20. I have a purpose

21. I have a bright and rewarding future ahead of me

22. I am uniquely designed with a master plan in mind

Image, restoring my self-image and developing a healthy identity

Now, create ten affirming statements of your own and begin saying them.

1. _____

2. _____

3. _____

4. _____

5. _____

6. _____

7. _____

8. _____

9. _____

10. _____

11. _____

Don't forget. Say your affirmations daily for twenty-one days or until they become automatic in your mind. You will know they are automatic when they come up without any intentional effort. You will find these words of affirmation rolling through your head without you even thinking about them.

Take it or leave it; learning to accept people for where they are

1. Have you had any new revelations about your past or present situation since reading this book?

2. Are you currently in an unhealthy relationship? If so, write about it. Why is it unhealthy?

Take it or leave it; learning to accept people for where they are

3. If you are currently in an unhealthy relationship, why have you chosen to stay?

4. Are there people in your life who you have chosen to believe more in their words than their behavior? Who are they?

Take it or leave it; learning to accept people for where they are

5. Now, list specific examples where their words and actions are not in alignment.

6. Now, based solely on behavior, is this person(s) safe or unsafe for you?

Take it or leave it; learning to accept people for where they are

7. If you are in an unhealthy relationship, what steps do you need to take to bring about change?

8. Take it or leave it; people are who they are

9. Who can you share your plan with?

Take it or leave it; learning to accept people for where they are

10. When and how will you share your plan?

11. Are there family members who need to know your plan? If yes, who are they? When and how will you tell them?

You shall know the truth and the truth will set you free

1. What did you see as a child?

2. What did you hear?

3. What did you feel?

You shall know the truth and the truth will set you free

4. How do you think witnessing family violence impacted you as a child?

5. Can you think of any lies you believed as a result of family violence or abuse?

6. What truths can you replace with these lies?

You shall know the truth and the truth will set you free

7. How do you think witnessing family violence or abuse impacted you as an adult?

8. Are there questions you have always wanted to ask your parents but were too afraid to ask?

You shall know the truth and the truth will set you free

9. If so, what has kept you from asking them?

10. Have you had any new revelations about your past since reading this book?

Witness

I call out to you now!

I cry out to you now!

Stand, be a witness!

You don't have to be silent anymore.

You don't have to carry the shame.

You don't have to carry their pain!

Hear the cry.... Let go of me!

Be free!!! I say be free!!

I speak to past pains and past memories.

I say you will not hold me.

I am FREE!!!

I choose freedom.

I choose life and liberty!

Yes! It is my choice now!

It is my voice now!

Shame, pain, and loneliness I take back the power I

gave to you.

This is well overdue. I no longer bow my knee to you.

I am free!

No more shackles, no more chains holding me.

I am free!

Part Four

Exposing the Demons on a National Level— Acknowledging the Generational Demons of Domestic Violence at Work in Our Nation

*Hillie and Lillian on their
wedding day July 18th, 1965*

CHAPTER FIFTEEN
DOMESTIC VIOLENCE: MYTH VERSUS TRUTHS

Violence was interwoven throughout our family foundation. I would like to shed some light on several extreme and devastating myths and truths using my families' violence experience as a foundation.

There is a great debate or statement made regarding abusive relationships. The statement on everyone's lips is, "if he really loved you, he would not abuse you." Well, for me it is a difficult question to answer because I can hear and understand critics' voices. In reflecting back on my parent's interactions when violence was not present and looking at old pictures of them, I can see they were very much in love. They had such love for each other.

Even today, I have watched my father and mother interact at special functions now more than 35 years later. My Dad will run and open the door for Mom, just like he did when we were growing up. He will serve her, getting her coat and helping her with it on. I believe my parents were deeply in love with each other at one time.

Still, I see they have a degree of love and concern for one another today. Through all that has transpired over the years, Mom found a way to forgive Dad and be cordial with him. So, I would conclude the violence offender can have love for the victim. It is possible they are actually in-love with the one they are abusing. However, they do not know how to act differently or at times simply choose not to express anger in a healthy way. Again, I see it as a sickness similar to an addiction or disease of the mind.

Something else to look at is if they are making the decision consciously or unconsciously. It is possible the violence offender could suffer from some type of mental illness, fear, and anxiety which could potentially drive them to unhealthy conclusions or suspicions and abnormal behavior. They could have a chemical imbalance in their brain or the individual could suffer from unresolved childhood trauma or issues. The violence offender could be reacting out of those hurts and wounds from childhood and possibly the only way they know how to resolve things is through violent behavior. In their family the only way things were resolved was through violence or abuse.

Today, Dad is a meek, mild and humble man. If you met him you would not suspect he could ever be violent. He has totally mellowed out over the years due to his conversion to Christ. In his younger days when he experienced hurt he always responded in anger. Now, if he is upset he breaks and cries. He is a man of tears. When I was growing up, I almost never saw my father cry. He to this day cannot comprehend why he was so violent toward my mother. He believed lies. He was always thinking Mom was seeing another man. Mom was very beautiful and petite. Another lie he believed in his mind was she just did not respond to him quickly enough, allowing other things and people to be more important than him.

We learned thirty-five years later there was a constant battle going on in his mind, a thought war taking place where Mom (or other women) was the enemy. Dad was plagued with insane thoughts. It was as if he was held captive or a prisoner in his mind, yet the bars were invisible. What he thought or felt was really happening appeared more real to him than reality. His reality was based on his own thinking; therefore, his thinking was holding him captive. The worst part was he never knew when his thoughts were reality or mere paranoia holding him captive. He could not discern when his thought prison doors were open or closing in on him. Nor, could he recognize when he stepped into his own cell, locking himself inside and lashing out at Mom or other women.

Like I said earlier, the majority of the time Dad could be one of the nicest men in the world. He could portray himself to us and others as a perfect gentleman, husband and father. He tried hard to act appropriately and be a good husband but there was a constant unseen war going on in his mind.

> **Myth**: If I am pregnant my abuser will not physically abuse me.

Truth: Women are often abused during pregnancy and miscarriage sometimes results.[10] [11]

My parents met at a friend's home and began dating. They dated for about a year and a half. They fell deeply in love and married on July 18, 1965. Mom conceived immediately and my brother Lorenzo was born less than one year later. During the first three months of their marriage things went very well. Then the abuse started. Even though my mother was pregnant, my father's rage was out of control and he abused Mom while she was pregnant.

When I was conceived it was a very difficult time. Mom had mustered up the courage once again to leave Dad. She had left him in times past only to return to him. He always begged and pleaded with her to return to him. Dad was quite the charmer and knew all the right things to say. Mom had planned to leave again when she found out she was pregnant with me. Due to all the violence she contemplated aborting me and leaving Dad for good. It was the late 1960's and abortions were illegal. Mom had heard of a doctor who did abortions and sought out information concerning him.

The landmark Roe v. Wade case had not made it to the courts. The case was not finalized until 1973. In the Roe v. Wade case the U.S. Supreme Court ruled abortion is a Constitutional right. Roe v. Wade overturned state laws against abortions.

Despite my father's abusive behavior, Mom could not go through with the illegal abortion. She decided to keep me. Looking back over my life and even while I was yet in my mother's womb, I can see where I was protected when I could not protect myself. And, I know there are many of us in the world who if it had not been for the mercy and grace of God, our mother would have aborted or miscarried us due to the physical, mental and emotional abuse experienced during pregnancy.

There have been many of us who have witnessed domestic violence and even experienced abuse or faced difficult circumstances which could have caused us to lose our lives or minds. The God of the Universe

---

10   Statistics Canada. (March 1994). Wife assault: The findings of a national survey. Juristat Service Bulletin, Vol. 14, No. 9, 1-22

11   Jaffe, P., Wolfe, D., & Wilson, S.K. (1990). Children of battered women, Thousand Oaks, CA: Sage.

kept us and protected us because He has a plan and divine purpose for our lives. He has uniquely designed each of us with a specific intended purpose in mind.

Unfortunately, some of us have lost our lives attempting to protect others when we were at the most vulnerable stage in our lives.

Myth: Children do not know domestic violence is taking place in the home.

Truth: Children from violent families can provide clinicians with detailed accounts of abusive incidents their parents never realized they had witnessed. (Peter Jaffe, David Wolfe and Susan Kaye Wilson (1990) Children of Battered Women. Newbury Park. CA: Sage Publications)[12]

I would guess that my earliest memory of domestic violence started at age three. Vividly, I can recall trying to stop my Dad from beating Mom at ages three, four, five and six years old. While my father was abusing my Mom I can recall getting caught between their legs, falling down, and getting back up to make every attempt to stop the violence.

For as long as I can remember, I knew my father to be a violent man. Actually, I was always very afraid of my father. But, when the violence was occurring there were two evils lurking or two lower evils to choose from. I could try to stop the insanity or cower and do nothing. I learned early to suppress fear and fight. Showing fear was not an option. Intuitively, I had to fight or try to do something no matter what was happening. It caused me more pain to see and know my mother was being abused than anything else, so most of the time I opted for trying to stop the violence. I was more than willing to take abuse, sometimes getting knocked down or hit in the cross fire. It was worth it, if it meant the violence perpetrated against Mom would be lessened, stopped or at least slowed down.

As I was writing this book I was talking to one of my friends about how much I can recall from childhood. I was telling her how amazed I am, in looking back that at a young age, I knew and understood what was going on and wanted to bring order to the chaotic situation. It just so happened there was domestic violence in my friend's first marriage and

---

12   http://www.speakout.org.za/about/child/child_impact.html (accessed November 27, 2008)

she told me a story about her son, Marcus. Marcus was between the ages of two and three years old and his father was a perpetrator of violence. One day his dad came home and my friend was busy talking on the telephone, it was late and dinner was late. So, the dad said to Marcus "your mom is so busy on the telephone running her mouth I bet she has not even fed you yet." My friend overheard them talking and heard Marcus respond, yes she fed me. In reality, she had not fed Marcus dinner. In an effort to protect his mom he lied. He had already seen enough of his father's violent behavior, so he quickly learned without anyone ever teaching him the lesson, do whatever it takes to attempt to control dad's rage.

> **Myth:** The abuser will not perpetrate violence towards our kids.

> **Truth:** Children in homes where domestic violence occurs are physically abused or seriously neglected at a rate 1500% higher than the national average in the general population. (National Women Abuse Prevention Project, Washington, D.C.)[13]

Consider these additional facts:

- Studies of abused children show that nearly half have mothers who are also abused, making wife abuse the single strongest identifiable risk for child abuse. (Lenore Walker, Ed.d "The Battered Woman Syndrome," New York: Springer Publishing Company, IDC. 1979)[14]

- In 1992 in the USA, an estimated 1,261 children died from abuse or neglect – more than three children died each day in the United States as a result of maltreatment. (National Committee for Prevention of Child Abuse, 1993)[15]

- Nearly 70% of children who go to shelters for battered women are victims of abuse or neglect. (Jean I Layzer. Barbara D. Goodson and Christine Delange "Children in Shelters", Response. Volume 9, Number 2, 1986)[16]

---

13   ibid
14   ibid
15   ibid
16   ibid

- Girls whose fathers batter their mothers are 6.5 times more likely to be sexually assaulted by their fathers than girls from non-violent homes. (perspectives on Wife Abuse Newbury Park, CA: Sage)[17]

My memories of being hit in the crossfire are not as clear as feeling and seeing the pain on my mother's face after she was abused. There were occasions where I or my brother was hit due to Dad's outrage. Today, I can still sense terror and pain as I recall some memories of witnessing domestic violence. Attempting to protect Mom was my way of being powerful and bringing order to chaos. I wanted to have some kind of power and control. I searched for some kind of peace among confusion. It was tormenting to my mind. Being powerless and helpless took my pain to a heightened level. The emotional pain outweighed physical pain. To say the least, the pain I felt witnessing domestic violence was indescribable. It was so traumatic seeing the two people you love the most fighting and hurting one another. In hindsight, I believe I suffered from some post traumatic stress as a child due to witnessing domestic violence.

Keep in mind this took place in the early 1970's in Chicago. During the very early 1970's women did not have laws on their side to protect them and shelters for battered women were nonexistent. The first battered women's shelter in the United States, Women's Advocates, was opened in St. Paul, Minnesota in 1974. This program is still in existence today. (NCADV VOICE Spring, 1994)[18]

There were times when the police were called; however, nothing was done to my father. I can recall one time standing by my mother's side and she was talking to the police. The officer just kept shaking his head. Mom was holding an ice pack to her swollen bruised eye and face. Dad had fled the scene prior to the arrival of the police. He did not go to jail on this occasion or any occasion. In fact, unless the police witnessed the violence, they considered domestic violence to be more of a civil matter.

Did you know?

- The first battered women's shelter opened in 1974 in the United States.

---

17   ibid
18   http://home.cybergrrl.com/dv/stat/statgen.html (accessed July 8, 2009)

- As of 1990, there were 1,500 shelters for battered women in the United States and there were 3,800 animal shelters (Schneider, 1990).[19]

- In 1999, the National Coalition Against Domestic Violence reported that the number of agencies providing services to battered women surpassed 2,000.[20]

- Number of animal shelters in the United States: Between 4,000 and 6,000 (HSUS estimate)[21]

Leaving the abuser is probably one of the most difficult things for the victim to do.

In most domestic violence situations the abuser has a loving side to them and that's what draws the victim and also makes it difficult for the victim to leave. In my mind as a child then and an adult today, I can only imagine how both Mom and I fantasized that somehow, someway, the chaos was going to stop and the monster would never return. In our hearts we hoped and believed the monster would go away permanently.

If you are caught in the cycle of abuse or know someone who is caught in the cycle, please know and understand, it usually takes several attempts to leave the abuser. It may even take a number of years. It is estimated 50 to 70 percent of women leave their abuser. However; leaving the abuser is not enough and does not stop the cycle of abuse. It is imperative for the victim, abuser and witnesses of abuse to get professional help to bring complete resolution, wholeness and healing. Otherwise the chance of repeating the cycle over and over again is great. Repeating the cycle is only one item at stake. The stakes become even higher once the victim attempts to leave the abuser because chances of the victim being murdered are greater at this volatile stage.

- In 1991, 28 percent of all female murder victims were slain by their husbands or boyfriends. [22]

---

19   ibid

20   http://www.findcounseling.com/journal/domestic-violence/battered-womens-shelters. html (accessed July 8, 2009) Saathoff, A., and E. Stoffel. *Community-Based Domestic Violence Services.* **The Future of Children: Domestic Violence and Children** (1999) 9(3):97-110.

21   http://www.hsus.org/pets/issues_affecting_our_pets/pet_overpopulation_and_ ownership_statistics/hsus_pet_overpopulation_estimates.html (accessed July 8, 2009)

22   Federal Bureau of Investigation. (1992) A Crime in the United States, 1991.@ Washington, D.C.

- Women who leave their batterers are at a 75 percent greater risk of being killed by the batterer than those who stay. [23]

Without the unconditional love and non-judgmental support of friends and family members it is almost impossible to escape. I emphasize non-judgmental support because most likely when someone starts passing judgment on the victim or shaming them for the place and position they are in, the victim will shut down and back up. The shame of being in an abusive relationship is incredible. Today, there is a greater awareness and more avenues of support. So, I suggest if one of your loved ones or friends are in a situation similar to this, to seek out ways you can support them in the process. Am I an advocate for leaving the abuser? Yes, and not necessarily. I think each situation is unique. To me it is more important to get help than to leave because if you do not get help, you are more likely to repeat the situation in some form or fashion just with a different partner. I have had a number of friends who were able to get help and the abuser changed. These couples have been able to go on and live healthy lifestyles.

Along with love and support from friends and family members I believe it takes faith and courage.

---

23   Hart, Barbara. (1988) A Domestic Violence Fact Sheet.@ National Coalition Against Domestic Violence. Washington, D.C.

CHAPTER SIXTEEN
THE DEMON'S IMPACT IN OUR NATION

Based on my study, family history and experience, I have gathered a number of findings which I would like to share. Number one, domestic violence for the most part is generational, meaning it's like a family heirloom is passed down from one generation to the next generation. The only difference is heirlooms have value and are passed down intentionally. While domestic violence is more like a generational curse. No one intentionally passes it down but it seems to make its way through the family lineage.

I have come to the conclusion that the abuse my father, mother and their siblings either witnessed or experienced had a profound effect on them as individuals. On my father's side of the family four out of five children have been in a violent relationship either as a perpetrator of violence or as a victim. On my mother's side of the family seven out of nine children have been involved in domestic violence either as a perpetrator or victim and all of them have been a witness to domestic violence as children. My conclusion is based on personal research and my family's experience. Here are just a few statistics I found to be alarming:

- Slightly more than half of female victims of intimate violence live in households with children under the age of 12.[24]

- Boys who have witnessed partner violence are much more likely to become batterers in their adult relationships than boys who have not had exposure to partner violence in their families. The data is mixed for girls. A child's exposure to the father abusing the

---

24   Bureau of Justice Statistics (BJS). May 2000. Intimate Partner Violence. Washington, DC: U.S. Department of Justice.

mother is the strongest risk factor for transmitting violent behavior from one generation to the next.[25]

- Children exposed to partner violence exhibit symptoms similar to children who are physically and sexually abused, including the perpetuation of violence.[26]

Domestic violence is usually generational so experiencing violence can seem like the norm. In my mother's lineage there have been at least three generations who have either experienced or witnessed domestic violence. It was nearly inevitable my mother would either be abused or end up in an abusive relationship because it was normal behavior in her family; she witnessed it and experienced it throughout her formative and adolescence years. Mom is the oldest of five girls in her family and each of her sisters at some point have been physically assaulted by either a boyfriend or husband. However, only one of them even attempted to report the violence to the authorities. Most immediate family members were aware of the abuse taking place and made attempts to intervene; however, intervention did not include reporting to authorities. Intervening usually meant becoming involved in the violence and oftentimes threatening or abusing the perpetrator.

Coincidently, of Mom's four brothers, the two eldest boys who witnessed the violence at a high degree have been in some type of relationship where there was violence. Now, the youngest two boys who have a vague recollection of domestic violence in the home have not perpetuated violence in their relationships.

While Mom's family life was extremely violent, it was something seldom if ever discussed as children. And, without a doubt counseling was never sought out or provided for the children or parents. Mom and her siblings would become adults before they ever really discussed episodes of abuse in detail. Unfortunately, the police were never called during episodes of abuse. Prior to the late 1970's there was not much support for women or children who were suffering from domestic violence. As abused women they learned to cover and tend to their own wounds. Unconsciously, they sent a subliminal message to their

---

25   US Department of Justice, Office of Justice Programs, Bureau of Just5ice Statistics Factbook: Violence by Intimates, March 1998,

26   Report of the American Psychological Association Presidential Task Force on Violence and the Family, APA, 1996.

children and others through their behavior saying this is normal, right and acceptable.

In Dad's case he also considered his home life as normal. So, the abuse, neglect and dysfunction never was discussed outside of family. It wasn't until one day we were watching the "Antwone Fisher Story" that my Dad really and truly realized the depth of dysfunction he grew up in. Seeing the movie seems to have taken away a level of shame and guilt from my father and he was able to freely admit what he had experienced was abuse and neglect.

Secondly, domestic violence is also cyclical, meaning it occurs in cycles and patterns. It is gradual and can go undetected in the beginning. It starts out slow and builds up momentum. Most perpetrators of abuse and abuse victims have either been victims of physical abuse themselves or witnessed domestic violence.

In Mom's case the violence did not start until after she had married my father. Usually domestic violence is cyclical and builds momentum as time goes on. There are warning signs which can be detected. Take my parents for example; while they were dating my father would become really angry at times and punch his fist up against a brick wall. Sometimes, he would punch the brick wall repeatedly until his hands would start to bleed. He would not hit Mom though he would inflict punishment on himself. This was a warning sign that something was drastically wrong with my father's psyche and emotions. He was obviously out of control and an abuser.

Mom did not see the warning signs which indicated Dad could and would eventually become violent toward her. When you have grown up in a violent environment, unless you are taught to look for the warning signs it is difficult to see them. I call them blind spots; it seems like you cannot see the forest for the trees. What is obvious to someone who grew up in a nonviolent environment is not generally visible to the person who is caught in the vicious generational cycle of domestic violence.

Thirdly, domestic violence scars in many places. Emotional, mental and physical scars are left behind on victims and perpetrators as well as those who witnessed domestic violence. In the article, The Power of Early Childhood, Bruce D. Perry, M.D., Ph.D said it best, "the human brain is an amazing and complex organ that allows each of us to think, feel and act. The qualities of humanity which have allowed us to create a democratic government, complex economies, astounding technologies and all other manifestations of our current society are mediated by the human brain.

In turn, these brain systems which allow us to think, feel, and act are shaped by experience. Furthermore, it is increasingly clear that the experiences of childhood act as primary architects of the brain's capabilities throughout the rest of life. These organizing childhood experiences can be consistent, nurturing, structured and enriched - resulting in flexible, responsible, empathic and intelligent contributors to society. Or, all too often, childhood experiences can be neglectful, chaotic, violent and abusive – resulting in impulsive, aggressive, remorseless, and intellectually-impoverished members of society. One set of experiences will produce tax-payers and one set of experiences will produce tax-consumers."

- Domestic violence and witnessing domestic violence can impact males and females dramatically different.

- Nearly one-third of American women will be abused by an intimate partner at some point in their lives.

- Each day, four women are murdered by husbands or boyfriends.

- Between 3.3 and 10 million children witness domestic violence annually.

- Children who witness abuse are at high risk for alcohol and drug use, depression, running away, violent behavior and suicide.

- Men who witness domestic violence as children are twice as likely to become abusers themselves.[27]

Fourth, domestic violence does not discriminate between social and economic classes. For the most part it does not discriminate between ethnic groups, with one exception, the African American race.

African Americans, especially African American women, suffer deadly violence from family members at rates decidedly higher than other racial groups in the United States. However, it is observed that

27   The Women's Safe House, http://www.twsh.org/Services.html

research concerning family violence among African Americans is inadequate.[28]

Overall, African Americans were victimized by intimate partners at significantly higher rates than persons of any other race between 1993 and 1998. Black females experienced intimate partner violence at a rate 35% higher than that of white females, and about 22 times the rate of women of other races. Black males experienced intimate partner violence at a rate of about 62% higher than that of white males and about 22 times the rate of men of other races.[29]

- The number one killer of African-American women between the ages 15-34 is homicide at the hands of a current or former intimate partner.[30]

- African-American women experience significantly more domestic violence than White women in the age group of 20-24. Generally, Black women experience similar levels of intimate partner victimization in all other age categories as compared to White women, but experience slightly more domestic violence. (Estimates are provided from the National Crime Victimization Survey, which defines an intimate partner as a current or former spouse, girlfriend, or boyfriend. Violent acts include murder, rape, sexual assault, robbery, aggravated assault, and simple assault.[31]

---

28   Callie Marie Rennison and Sarah Welchans, U.S. Dep't of Just., NCJ 178247, Intimate Partner Violence (2000), available at http:www.ojp.usdoj.gov/bjs/pub/ascii/ipv.txt

29   Callie Marie Rennison and Sarah Welchans, U.S. Dep't of Just., NCJ 178247, Intimate Partner Violence (2000), available at http:www.ojp.usdoj.gov/bjs/pub/ascii/ipv.txt

30   Africana Voices Against Violence, Tufts University, Statistics, 2002, www.ase.tufts.edu/womenscenter/peace/africana/newsite/statistics.htm

31   Callie Marie Rennison, U.S. Dep't of Just., NCJ 187635, *Intimate Partner Violence and Age of Victim, 1993-1999*, at 4, (2001) available at http://www.opj.usdoj.gov/bjs/abstract/ipva99.htm

CHAPTER SEVENTEEN
CHARACTERISTICS OF A
BATTERER

Initially, the batterer will try to explain his behavior as signs of love and concern but as time goes on, the behaviors become more severe. He may not have all of these characteristics[32]:

- Jealousy
- Controlling behavior
- Quick involvement
- Unrealistic expectations
- Isolation
- Blames others for his problems
- Blames others for his feelings
- Hypersensitivity
- Cruelty to animals or children
- "Playful" use of force during sex
- Verbal abuse
- Rigid sex roles
- Dr. Jekyll and Mr. Hyde personality
- Threats of violence
- Breaking or striking objects
- Any force during an argument
- Objectification of women
- Low self-esteem
- Tight control over finances
- Minimization of violence
- Manipulation through guilt
- Close minded

32   http://www.sccadvasa.org/articles/82.pdf (accessed July 8, 2009)

The contrast between a perpetrator's public image and private behavior with the abused partner sometimes appears confusing and contradictory. Perpetrators are extremely proficient at disguising their abusive behaviors in order to appear socially proper. For example, jealousy that turns to abusive rage or abuse in private may look like concern and sensitivity in public. Traits that may be interpreted as protective, caring aspects of a perpetrator's personality may in actuality be possessiveness, manipulation, power and control. Many times, perpetrators are able to control their hostile expressions of power and control until after courtship, marriage or the establishment of other committed living arrangements.

The best way I can describe this is like holding a balloon under water in a swimming pool. You can hold the balloon or ball under water for so long, but eventually the balloon will push to the surface because of the pressure inside the balloon or because you become tired of holding the balloon down. Therefore, the balloon surfaces until enough pressure is applied to hold it down again.

RECOVERY &
WHOLENESS BOOKS

Do you want Renesia Martin to speak to your group or event? Contact Renesia directly by emailing: renesiamartin@gmail.com

For information on childhood domestic violence, visit www.CDV.org

Need more information?

National Domestic Violence Hotline: 800-788-SAFE. This is a twenty-four-hour referral service for domestic violence shelters and therapists specializing in the treatment of abusive relationships.

www.ingramcontent.com/pod-product-compliance
Lightning Source LLC
Chambersburg PA
CBHW031249090426
42742CB00007B/374